Carl Van Vechten

and the Twenties

CARL
VAN VECHTEN
AND THE
TWENTIES

by Edward Lueders

UNIVERSITY OF NEW MEXICO PRESS

1955

CARL VAN VECHTEN, PHOTOGRAPHED BY MAN RAY, IN PARIS

FOR MY MOTHER AND MY FATHER

BY A VERY PLEASANT COINCIDENCE, the publication of this book falls in the spring of 1955, the season and the year in which Carl Van Vechten celebrates his seventy-fifth birthday.

This fact can help explain the nature of my book, for, although it features biographical material, it is not a biography of Carl Van Vechten. Neither can it qualify as a critical study of his works, although it discusses and evaluates all of Van Vechten's books. Specifically, my book stops at 1932 but Van Vechten did not. At that time he announced his retirement as an author of books, but, in the years since, he has continued his active role as a vital observer, contributor, and participant in the arts and in American life.

Van Vechten's seven novels, his ten volumes on music and the arts, and his two books about cats all appeared between the First World War and the Great Depression. The purpose of my study, then, was determined by the nature of Van Vechten's books and the times that produced them.

Perhaps I can describe this book in the parlance of advertising as a "package deal," designed to be both functional and attractive. Our knowledge of the Twenties is incomplete unless it includes the books and the activities of Carl Van Vechten. At the same time, a discussion of his books is inevitably a discussion of the wonderful, hectic high life of the Twenties. Thus, while my book is neither a complete social history of the Twenties nor a full critical biography of Carl Van Vechten, it is meant to be something of both. The two subjects are natural complements: the Twenties are viewed through the books of Van Vechten, and Van Vechten is seen in relation to the era for which and about which he wrote.

My indebtedness to those who have seen me through the preparation of this book is inadequately represented by any catalogue of their names. To Dr. George Arms of the University of New Mexico I owe my initial momentum. He and his colleagues, Drs. C. V. Wicker, Hugh M. Miller, George W. Smith, and T. M. Pearce assisted me at many stages of the work. I appreciate the service and the kindness of Helen McIntyre of the University of New Mexico Library, Rosemary Demaree, then of the Purdue University Library, Robert W. Hill of the New York Public Library, Donald Gallup, Editor of the Yale University Library Gazette, and Florence Batson, for permission to reprint certain materials published by the Macmillan Company.

I am most grateful to Mabel Dodge Luhan of Taos and Cora Headington of Corrales, New Mexico, who read the initial manuscript and offered valuable suggestions.

During the production of the book, Roland F. Dickey has been a rare combination of good companion and creative editor.

Above all, I am indebted to Carl Van Vechten for accepting so cordially both me and my project, and for making available to me, with only the vaguest idea of the use to which they might be put, materials which would have been difficult or impossible to acquire without his personal aid.

To my wife, Judy, who served with amazing equanimity as her husband's typist and consultant, my gratitude is perhaps best expressed by my customary tacit admiration.

EDWARD LUEDERS

Albuquerque
February 14, 1955

I. THE TWENTIES:

Preludes and Patterns

DURING WORLD WAR II, John O'Hara, himself a veteran of the social and literary wars of the Twenties, asked rhetorically, "If I were to get on the squawk-box and say to Fighting 18: 'Now hear this: Carl Van Vechten is aboard and will be pleased to answer any questions'— would the fighter pilots know what the hell to ask him?" O'Hara indicated his doubt and added, ". . . you might care to know that Van Vechten's slim volumes had a little of the same screwy life that was caught by Fitzgerald in *The Great Gatsby*."

Actually, Van Vechten's volumes are not slim, and they contain considerably more than a little of "the same screwy life" caught by F. Scott Fitzgerald in *The Great Gatsby*. But O'Hara's estimate of their neglect, just two decades after their popularity was assumed by the reading public in the phrase "The Van Vechten Vogue," is correct. Perhaps their very contemporaneousness with the times that produced them is chiefly responsible for their rapid decline in notoriety (a more fitting word than "reputation" when discussing any aspect of their day).

Generally, the volumes that came from the pen of Carl Van Vechten between 1915 and 1932 have been relegated to the lists of authors and titles compiled for studies of our literature in the Twenties. The few literary historians who have discussed these books customarily have cited them as sophisticated and symptomatic addenda to the period. As the Twenties come more clearly into focus, however, it becomes evident that there was much in both the life and the work of Van Vechten which was source as well as symptom.

CARL VAN VECHTEN, PHOTOGRAPHED BY SAUL MAURIBER, AFTER A PHOTOGRAPH OF SALVADOR DALI BY HALSMAN, NEW YORK, 1944

The writings of Van Vechten offer to the readers of a later age insight into the arts, the literature, and the society of America in the Nineteen Twenties. Whether his readers seek data or diversion matters little—these are inseparable elements in any of his works. The parade of Van Vechten's nineteen books capering through the rowdy avenues of the Twenties presents a tangible review of an irrepressible era.

1. THE SOCIAL ABERRATIONS of the Twenties make a gaudy catalogue. The decade had many aspects of a national debauch, yet the national conviction of well-being persisted. The ten-year glitter may have been one of fool's gold, but the glitter was no less attractive for that. Even those who recognized the metal of the times for what it was, were often content and proud to harmonize with their surroundings, admitting with T. S. Eliot's prophetic Prufrock that they were "almost, at times, the Fool." The capitalization made all the difference, for wasn't the Fool a professional jester behind whose antics and whirling words lay a sage commentary on the scene? If, as Walter Lippmann proclaimed by adapting Aristophanes to his generation in *A Preface to Morals,* Whirl was king, Carl Van Vechten was—among other things—its Fool.

Seldom has a distinctive era in American life been so sour in its inception, so rampant in its course, so complete in its collapse. Economically, the Twenties began with the sudden slump in the price of securities on the New York Stock Exchange in November, 1919, heralding the end of the war boom which had seen the country through the Wilson era. The finale came in October, 1929, with the catastrophic climax to bull market speculation. Politically the era began by turning almost militantly on the Wilsonian idealism to which the nation had clung so fervently through the war. The popular alternative was a return to "normalcy" under Harding, long a servant of special interests, and his successor, Calvin Coolidge, who epitomized his philosophy of government in the assertion that "The business of the United States is business," a statement that tried to be

Carl Van Vechten

a cathartic but proved to be a conundrum. The conclusion of the era found the nation just as militant against "normalcy" and big business, symbolized by Herbert Hoover's continuation of the Republican regime, as it had been against Wilsonian idealism ten years before. By the time the Greek tragedy of Hoover's gallant stand had run its course in 1932, the nation brought the merry-go-round of the Twenties to a full circle by returning the reins to the Democrats and Franklin Roosevelt's promise of a New Deal.

Sandwiched in between these events was a decade of social and intellectual revolt that moved from disillusion to dissolution in its search for the elusive goal of self-realization. Beginning in the dull resentment of postwar reality, the general atmosphere of the Twenties grew in cynicism, lawlessness, intolerance, and bitterness. The spiritual strength and security which had bolstered generations of Americans was untenable to vast numbers who searched for intellectual balance in a world of cold reality, with the beam of twentieth-century science revealing strange, uncomfortable corners of the universe and the soul. A generation which, in the words of Joseph Wood Krutch, reviewing its symptoms at the decade's end, had "awakened to the fact that both the ends which its fathers proposed to themselves and the emotions from which they drew their strength seem irrelevant and remote," faced the need of a new intellectual code, a new reason for existence. The search turned its range from eternity to the moment, symbolized most picturesquely, perhaps, by the sophisticate's ceaseless quest throughout the Prohibition era for an unholy grail. "The Lost Generation," Gertrude Stein's familiar phrase for the authors, artists, and intellectuals of the Twenties, contains an ambiguity which doubles its aptness: lost as a person who cannot find his way and lives in confusion, and (one wonders how consciously Miss Stein was aware of it) also in the sense of one lost to salvation, abandoned to sin.

Much of the American's world was whittled down to the moment. The term *modern* (which, like everything else, became dated and gave way to *modernistic*) serves as well as any for a keynote. More than ever before, the *new*—the thing of the latest moment—became almost violently desirable and important. Science and business combined to subdivide time and space in everyday life through the production and sales of automobiles, airplanes, radios and the movies. Business, discovering that its goal of ever-increasing production-and-expansion depended largely on this public deification of the latest thing, bombarded the willing populace with the assertion that every change was progress, that everything new was bigger and/or better. The essential ingredients of revolt and experiment in the atmosphere of the Twenties served as catalytic agents leading to some of the most impressive accomplishments and some of the most grotesque excesses achieved in the nation's history. Everything, good or bad, seemed to make its appearance headlong.

There was much to offset the social failures of the Twenties, the symptomatic irresponsibility present at all levels of society, the farce of Prohibition and its fruits of lawlessness, the drunkenness, the intellectual dishonesty, the gross immorality, and the sophomoric indignity of a nervous society inclined to notoriety for its own sake. Balancing the Prohibition laws was the Nineteenth Amendment, which extended the democratic franchise to women and dealt the most substantial blow in our history to the double standard. Commercial expansion raised America to a level of production more commensurate with its tremendous potential. The comforts and conveniences of the common man multiplied more rapidly than during any previous period, and his opportunities for recreation were more varied and readily available than ever before.

Curiously, though, and consistent with an age that featured paradox on every hand, these gains were responsible for some of the most notorious excesses of the time. Women, granted the right to vote, demanded and took their new freedom wherever they could find it, and the scandalous flapper with her mannish clothes and conscious impertinence emerged. In the flush of expansion, business over-produced, over-reached itself, standardized its demands for quantity buying and selling, and supported its aims and means through the ballyhoo of that monster with head in the legendary position of an ostrich and arms working like an octopus: advertising. The conveniences offered the masses, coupled with the easy credit of installment buying, hastened the bankruptcy of the country by hamstringing the working man, who found himself forever paying for

6   *Carl Van Vechten*

last month's washing machine, automobile, radio, or house furnishings out of this month's pay check. His recreations led to a new kind of national appetite for games and fads, for physical and mental exercises that laid him open to any charlatan willing to go big-time, and, above all, for celebrities, the kings and queens of the movies, sports, and the radio.

Even the arts, which were expanding along with everything else in the growth of the Twenties, displayed the excess bred of national demand for novelty. With popular taste following notoriety, availability, and ballyhoo, it is not surprising that so much ephemera and so much charlatanism found a ready market. More remarkable, however, are the solid, lasting contributions to the arts which remain now that the ephemera has had its day. Out of the social and intellectual revolt of the times came a widespread release in the arts which America and Americans had never before accomplished. Much of it was due to expansion, both geographical and intellectual. Sophistication demanded a more mature approach to art, and experiment required a knowledge of what had been attempted. The war years had left Americans with a new consciousness, in many instances first-hand, of the European continent. A society tired of being contained, rebellious at being restrained, found its spokesmen in artists, musicians, and writers who helped it feel modern, new, different and revolutionary. The infiltration of international culture became vital to an American society ready to replace traditional provincialism with something more cosmopolitan. American artists discovered that a more cultivated sensitivity was possible once the provincial barriers were down, and the spirit of cultural revolt and experiment opened an approach to them. The American audience for literature, art, music, and the theatre grew in proportion as these arts supplied it with an initiation into the sophisticated elect. The electric age was upon us and the public was willingly accepting a national shock treatment.

Among the artists, writers, and musicians, however, the revolt had the character of a mission as well as a diversion. The ferment was not as new as the public believed; it had merely been awaiting the ripening of the time. John Chamberlain in his *Farewell to Reform* (1932), caught the scene in a brief paragraph:

When Woodrow Wilson took the oath of office in 1913, the movement had gathered something approaching a real momentum. Mencken and Nathan, their brows touched by the consecrating wands of Percival Pollard and James Huneker, were beginning to work in tandem. Insatiable young souls just out of Yale, Paul Rosenfeld and Waldo Frank, had caught a glimpse of an America transformed by art from the camera work of Alfred Stieglitz. Boys and girls who had seen Isadora Duncan dance, who had listened to Emma Goldman define anarchism, who had caught the infectious dental grin of Roosevelt, became sick of the tepid loyalties of their fathers. Decorum was no word for the day.

It was on such a stage that Carl Van Vechten, first as a critic and later as a novelist, aware of both the mission and the diversion and equally aware of himself, played his role.

2. VAN VECHTEN'S FIRST BOOK was published when he was thirty-five, but the years which preceded its appearance were active and adventurous. Many of the essays in his last book, *Sacred and Profane Memories* (1932), are reminiscences of these earlier years, and one of them, "Notes for an Autobiography," sketches in six pages some significant details of his personal history up to 1923.

Carl Van Vechten was born in Cedar Rapids, Iowa, on June 17, 1880. His family, a respected part of the community, offered a more substantial environment for a son who "cannot remember the time when he was not trying to write" than one might picture in nineteenth-century Cedar Rapids. Van Vechten recalls that "The Woman's Journal always lay on our sitting-room table, along with Harper's Weekly and the Atlantic Monthly." His mother, who had known Lucy Stone in college, was an early champion of women's suffrage and an occasional force for the improvement of taste and cultural facilities in her sphere—"She was also responsible for the public library in our town." His father had been a subscriber to the *Atlantic Monthly* since its first issue, and once helped an Iowa friend found a school for Negroes in Mississippi.[1]

One of Van Vechten's most charming essays, "The Tin Trunk" in *Sacred and Profane Memories,* utilizes a box of mementos to touch off reflections of the author's family and personal life in Cedar Rapids. The memories are set down with the grace, the sentiment, and the calm poignancy that only time and distance can inspire. In daguerreotype tones the essay pictures his boyhood scenes, and many of the details blend neatly and comfortably with the later career of the writer and with his books. What is missing, however, is the author's own restlessness, that claustrophobia of the spirit which demanded expansion, experiment, and esoteric experience instead of routine comfort and provincial conformity. Many of the memories returning most pleasantly are those which led away from Cedar Rapids.

Music was an accepted part of the Van Vechten family life. The three children all played instruments. Carl, the youngest, and his sister Emma, whom he remembers as "an excellent pianist," both played their mother's old Gilbert square rosewood grand; and Van Vechten pictures his brother Ralph, who was eighteen years his senior, as "a thin serious-looking boy . . . who passed his spare time in practicing the violin and in printing." Books take their place in these memories, beginning with J. T. Trowbridge and Horatio Alger Jr. and moving through Dickens, Richard Harding Davis, Mark Twain, Shakespeare, and Ibsen, eventually including *What Maisie Knew,* Daudet's *Sapho,* and two books that "made an indelible impression" on him: *The Confessions of a Young Man* and *Plays Pleasant and Unpleasant.* Van Vechten's interest in the theatre grasped any part of it which filtered through to Iowa. "One of my earliest memories," he has written elsewhere, "is connected with an amateur production of *The Sorcerer* [the Gilbert and Sullivan opera] at Greene's Opera House, Cedar Rapids, Iowa. I could not have been more

1. The school is at Piney Woods, Mississippi. Laurence Jones, the Negro friend from Marshalltown, Iowa, is still its director.

than seven or eight years old." Other shows which played Cedar Rapids on tour were a part of his fare, while pictures and posters of theatrical artists comprised one of his earliest collections.

When Van Vechten left his Iowa home for the newly endowed University of Chicago, Cedar Rapids slipped quickly into the background. The move signalled his release from provincialism and his initiation into the first stage of cosmopolitanism. New York and Europe, especially and ultimately Paris, were easy, almost predestined steps after Chicago. But Iowa never quite left Van Vechten. The man is too genuinely cosmopolitan by nature and inclination to be spoken of as transplanted from Midwestern soil to the common earth of Western culture. And such a figure of speech is too heavy and dramatic for a growth which came naturally, almost inevitably. Yet there is the recognizable stamp of America on his life and work; however widely he roams, however Gallic, British, or individual are his overtones, the American is still in him. The process was one of cross-fertilization rather than transplanting; the result is more a fleur-de-lis grafted on an Iowa cornstalk (such a combination would serve Van Vechten's taste for strange contrasts and novel assortments) than any series of single plants. Indeed, the emblematic decoration on the cover and the title page of *Sacred and Profane Memories* can be seen as representing such a union—sheaves of corn bound below the middle, flaring out a bit at the base with cascading arms bending down from above.

A number of essays attest to his later fondness for the years in Iowa, and *The Tattooed Countess* offsets its satire of the smallness and hypocrisy of Maple Valley, Iowa, with a genuine feeling for the innate charm and color of the locale. Mabel Dodge Luhan, writing of her early acquaintance with Van Vechten, comments on this affection which could be realized only when he was assured of his escape. "Everything that took Carl farther away from Cedar Rapids was desirable to him at that time, though later he became conscious of his inexterminable love for it, and for old brick houses set in lawns, with rep-covered furniture and square pianos in them, and he capitulated and reproduced such a room in his apartment."

In Chicago all three of Van Vechten's professional careers as music critic, novelist, and (after 1932) photographer, were nurtured. As a student at the University of Chicago, Van Vechten specialized in English under Robert Morss Lovett (who remained a good friend and whom Van Vechten refers to as "the best teacher I ever had"), William Vaughn Moody, and Robert Herrick, the novelist. He wrote for campus publications and poured his energies into college themes, the latter now secured in the New York Public Library to be withheld during their author's lifetime. Several of these themes, it has been revealed, deal with Negroes, a subject which has held Van Vechten's interest and enthusiasm throughout his life.

Music remained an active hobby during the seven years spent in Chicago. As a performer, he participated in duet sessions with other pianists or with violinists; as a listener, he gained an orchestral education from Theodore Thomas and the Chicago Symphony, an organization notable for the introduction of new music into its concert programs, a practice generally avoided by conductors of that time.

Upon receiving his Ph.B. degree, Van Vechten stayed in Chicago as a reporter for Hearst's *Chicago American*. He wrote little for the newspaper, however, his assignments being the spot coverage of news stories which he telephoned to the rewrite desk. Before his departure from the *American*, his duties had been largely changed to collecting photographs of subjects in the news. Van Vechten was so satisfactory at this that he was kept at it almost exclusively. But Chicago was merely the necessary limbo between Cedar Rapids and New York. In 1906, after seven years of education, both formal and informal, Van Vechten moved on to the city with which, together with Paris, his name is most closely associated.

New York accepted him well and established him quickly as a music critic. He sold a paper on the opera *Salome* to Theodore Dreiser's *Broadway Magazine,* and shortly thereafter was hired by the *New York Times* as assistant to its venerable music critic, Richard Aldrich. By 1907, Van Vechten had satisfied a number of his major ambitions. He was a citizen of the sophisticated society of New York, far removed from the provincialism of Cedar Rapids, and he was a successful writer, a music critic and a contributor to the cosmopolitan journals of his day.

From that time on, the record is crowded with activity and accomplishment. His association with the *Times* as critic was long and fruitful, including a year's service as Paris correspondent for that newspaper. Travel abroad satisfied a thirst for new experience and a further retreat from Philistia. In 1913 he became drama critic for a short stay with the *New York Press*. A year later he was again abroad, caught in the hectic opening scenes of the war in Europe. Jobless in 1915, he put together the manuscript of his first book, *Music After the Great War*. Through the next seventeen years—his last volume appeared in 1932—he engaged himself in the steady production of books of critical essays, books about cats, and his seven novels. Until the publication of his first novel, *Peter Whiffle*, in 1922, however, his readers knew him as a refreshingly individual critic of music and the arts.

3. THE PURPOSE AND THE METHOD of Van Vechten's criticism are stated in two passages from his early work. In 1917 he wrote:

> Musical criticism has two purposes: one, and perhaps the most important, is to entertain the reader; because criticism, like any other form of literature, should stand by itself and not lean too heavily on the matter of which it treats; the other is to interest the reader in music, or in books about music, or in musicians. Criticism can be informing without being pedantic; it can prod the pachydermal hide of a conservative old fogey concert-goer without deviating from the facts.

In an essay of 1919, he added after some good-natured ridicule of critics who propose rules by which art can be measured, "It seems to me that the 'impressionistic' critic who expresses his personal preferences is much more likely to light up his subject. He is not tied down by a theory." These declarations come as close as any to the critical creed which Van Vechten consistently applied in the discussion of any art.

Such a creed was not exactly new, but it was particularly suitable for a critic writing in an age which was just discovering Continental innovations in the arts, ridiculing the academic platitudes of the "professors," and turning avidly to anything which would lead to an individual sophistication of taste. Some of Van Vechten's battles had been fought and won by James Huneker and Lawrence Gilman before he entered the fray, and the odds against their "impressionistic" criticism had dropped considerably by the time Van Vechten's books sought a reading audience. It was still the same war on stuffiness and blind tradition in 1915 and 1920 as it had been in 1900. The difference was that a part of the wilderness was ready to listen to the voices now. The iconoclast was in vogue; revolt and experiment had appointed him.

Earlier American critics, however, had established the literary quality of our music criticism. Between the time of John S. Dwight's *Journal of Music,* founded in 1852, and the era of such sophisticated essayists as Huneker and Van Vechten, our writers on music maintained standards of literary expression even when their judgments on music were unimpressive. By the turn of the century, the Old Guard of Henry E. Krehbiel, Henry T. Finck, William Foster Apthorp, W. J. Henderson, and Van Vechten's mentor of the *Times,* Richard Aldrich, had written solid, substantial books, essays, and reviews calculated to educate the American public in matters musical. They were properly dignified by Oscar Thompson with the collective title, "The American School of Criticism."

But the points of irritation for a critic like Van Vechten lay in the terms of such a title: American, (isolation, ingrown tradition, provincialism) and School (judgment according to predetermined artistic formula, "theory," narrowness, rigid consistency, suspended animation). The arts were alive to Carl Van Vechten and his writing sought to re-create that life. Sentimental or informative exposition was an insufficient method in itself. What was needed, and what his essays supplied, was the vitality, the aesthetic evocation of the artistic experience itself.

Paul Henry Lang has written suggestively about this matrix method, and the somewhat mystical quality of his words can be resolved in the example of Van Vechten's essays: "The critic is a man in whom the spiritual content of a work of art becomes an experience of vital force. This experience acquires in his writing a life of its own, it becomes a profession of faith, a point of view."

There is, unfortunately, no objective method of accurately determining the influence of a critic, but there is presumptive evidence that as a critic Van Vechten was no idle singer of an empty day. He was anything but idle, his day was as crowded with activity as any in our history, and the perspective of thirty years shows him to be either an influence or a prophet in American music—probably both. His was the loudest, most insistent voice calling for recognition of the musical revolution. At a time when the names of Stravinsky, Satie, Ornstein, and Schoenberg were unknown to the many and anathema to the remaining few, Van Vechten was a defender of their experiments and a champion of their art. The outspoken heresy of such advocacies now that the cause has been long won, is difficult to appreciate.

Van Vechten's record of "firsts" is impressive. His extensive and scholarly study, *The Music of Spain,* was the first book in our language to give the subject general coverage, and the only ambitious treatment of Spanish music in English for many years. He was the first to write at any length and with informed appreciation of the Russian Ballet, the musical activities of the foreign language theatre in New York, and the new theories of stage decoration for opera stemming from Adolphe Appia and Gordon Craig.

Above all, he introduced into his essays the attitude toward music-at-large in America which, with its spread both horizontally and vertically through the media of the phonograph, radio, sound movies, and popular orchestras, has become the only whole approach to the subject. Van Vechten wrote with enthusiasm and imagination of the opportunities suggested by music in the early movie houses, of the promise in American musicals and vaudeville, of music in its more natural settings away from the artificialities of the concert hall, and of American jazz, which—

although he granted it might not be all we might wish for—constituted for him the best hope in sight for a distinctive American music. He fought continually the misconception that because anything was entertaining or popular—or both—it should receive critical scorn. In this respect he was the only critic of his generation to anticipate both in spirit and in prophecy the metamorphosis in our music after the Twenties. Since then, the development of electronic sound reproduction and a tremendous increase in musical activities of all sorts have produced such a variety in musical fare for our everyday listening that the traditional gap between classical or serious music and popular music is to be found only by the static traditional ear.

Van Vechten's remaining contribution to music criticism is perhaps his most characteristic. Always alive to the great moments in art, he led his readers to the performer, the interpreter who gave body, personality, and reality to an artistic creation. This appreciation of performance as the fulfillment of conception is typical of Van Vechten's search for animation, for uniqueness in art. In terms of the society of the times, it may be viewed as a prelude to the celebrity-worship of the Twenties, the deification of the glamorous, successful personality—but to Van Vechten it was more than this. In the interpretations of Mary Garden, Waslav Nijinsky, Olive Fremstad and the others who gratified his eye and ear, he found art in motion, realized and *given*.

> There is an *au delà* to all great interpretative art, something that remains after story, words, picture, and gesture have faded vaguely into that storeroom in our memories where are concealed these lovely ghosts of ephemeral beauty, and the artist who is able to give us this is blessed even beyond his knowledge, for to him has been vouchsafed the sacred kiss of the gods. This quality cannot be acquired, it cannot even be described, but it can be felt. With its beneficent aid the interpreter not only contributes to our pleasure, he broadens our horizon, adds to our knowledge and capacity for feeling.

Possessed with such sentiment for the performer, he was lavish in his praise of great interpretation, but not indiscriminate. He was prepared to be generous in accepting imperfections, but he lamented flaws that prevented a complete creation on the stage. His judgment of performances was consistent with his taste in all art, and in life. If it was wholly alive, striking and memorable in breadth, nuance, and uniqueness, it was a great and cherished experience for Van Vechten.

4. *FICTION IN THE EARLY DECADES* of the century followed three major trends, each of which reflected the shifting temper of American society.

Through a quarter century the public appetite for reform was whetted by the writings of the muckrakers and the literary agents of social consciousness who followed them. The early exploitation of public corruption and scandal by writers whom Theodore Roosevelt likened to the man with the muck rake in *Pilgrim's Progress* cleared a path for novelists to follow. Ida M. Tarbell's 1902 account of the dubious practices of big business, *The History of the Standard Oil Company*, sounded its echoes in the fictionalized crusades of Upton Sinclair, notably his exposure of the meat-packing industry in *The Jungle*. The political graft and corruption in positions of civic responsibility revealed in Lincoln Steffen's *The Shame of the Cities* was utilized thematically by Brand Whitlock in *The Thirteenth District*, by David Graham Phillips in *The Master Rogue* and *The Plum Tree*, and the competitive harshness of metropolitan life was explored in the novels of Robert Herrick and Theodore Dreiser. Ray Stannard Baker's *The Railroads on Trial* had its counterpart in *The Octopus* of Frank Norris.

The avid socialism of Jack London seeped into his novels of adventure. Sinclair Lewis and others (Van Vechten among them) turned their satire on the provincialism and hypocrisy of Small Town America. Through the Twenties and into the depression years of the Thirties the novel of social protest was kept alive by writers like Dos Passos and Steinbeck to expand into the exposition of world socio-political ideologies in our harrowing mid-century years.

A second trend, often found in combination but distinguished by its quality of personal introspection, gave literary rebirth to the estranged, disillusioned, highly sensitive individual in fiction. The post-war cynicism of bright young men was channeled into brittle, discouraged sagas of self-seeking. The microcosm of the self, insecure and distrustful of an antagonistic macrocosm, turned in upon itself for reassurance and wrote of its vain struggle for balance and fulfillment. Futility had been the fruit of World War I idealism. The disillusioned intellectuals of America, for a vicarious realization of their own mixture of hope and dismay, turned to these chronicles of the defiant individual caught in the tragedy of existence. E. E. Cummings' *The Enormous Room,* Dos Passos' *Three Soldiers,* and Hemingway's war-born novels, all drew on the scenes of the War itself as the backdrop to the personal tragedy. Others moved the drama closer home, depicting the dispossession of the sensitive soul by his own native environment. Floyd Dell's *Moon Calf* bewailed the fate of the young man of vague genius struggling in the sloughs of provincial mediocrity and his own inarticulate superiority. F. Scott Fitzgerald's *This Side of Paradise*—an amazingly adolescent attempt in the light of its reputation and its author's later accomplishments—might have been just another novel in the genre had it not played so neatly into the hands and imaginations of an American public eager to regain the release offered by the easy sophistication of youth, and just as eager to shock itself in the process.

Ultimately, these ingrown odysseys of the sensitive soul searching for identity and fulfillment explored tributaries which spilled over into the sprawling reservoir of Thomas Wolfe.

The contribution of these novels to modern literature has been rich and significant. They have given us a philosophy of the individual which has served simultaneously the needs of personal autonomy and sublimated release in our intellectual conscience. They have given us an intimate record of some of the most remarkable personalities we have produced, and have revealed a sensitivity in the American fiber rarely articulated in earlier periods.

But a curious flaw, discernible in the group more than in any single volume, adds an ironic footnote to their contribution. While they draw their strength from the cold treatment of tragic reality, the warmth of their subjective yearning constitutes a new brand of sentimentality. They display masochistic satisfaction in beating their sensitive heads against an insensitive wall, and recording all the details of their excruciation. They crowd their pages with so many negative doubts that they some-times delude themselves through some mystic personal algebra that they have arrived at something positive. And they are serious, with a serious-ness that can never let a moment of pleasure go without its burden of tragic melancholy. Their impact is disturbing, provoking, and deep, so much so as to stand badly in need of either the allegorical molds of a Melville or the relief of the wit and comic sense of a Shakespeare.

The third trend in fiction is generally accorded the misleading adjectives *light, escapist,* or *romantic.* While each of these accurately designates one aspect of the genre, all three together fail to classify fully the novels of such artists in prose as Van Vechten, Joseph Hergesheimer, James Branch Cabell, and Elinor Wylie. *Charming,* in the sense of a spell-binding personality, would have to be a fourth adjective, for these writers believed with Van Vechten's Peter Whiffle that "it was the charm of David which had slain the ugly giant, just as charm always kills ugli-ness." The legacy which they brought to an American fiction devoted to realism and naturalism was the legacy of style, of creative imagination, of the unique personality, of artifice, and of sophisticated prose palatable to the literary gourmet—but too over-civilized and precocious a dish for the meat and potatoes reader. This is not to say that the staples were lack-ing. Robert Frost has said that some writers offer a good deal of dirt with the potato but he prefers his scraped clean. To continue his figure, we can say that these writers served their potato not only clean but cooked with a chef's consummate care. It was still a potato.

This care for style flavored the American fiction of the period with the principle of art-for-art's-sake, the Continental overtones of which had never been so widely heard in America before. It balanced with an entertaining flair for whimsy, wit, and fantasy the solemnity and nervous immediacy of the social protests and the sensitive egos in fiction. Even when it commented on society and probed its weaknesses—as it did in all of Van Vechten's and Cabell's novels—*it enjoyed itself*. These authors intended to be sophisticated and entertaining and they were; but the vitality and wit of their art was sometimes mistaken for mere playfulness and frivolity. Speaking from the viewpoint of the *New Masses,* Joseph Freeman wrote, "Carl Van Vechten prattles upper-class nonsense for the amusement of our nouveaux riches. James Branch Cabell plagiarizes from a thousand healthy folk fantasies and weaves the results into flashy patterns for the same nouveaux riches." Van Vechten, speaking through Campaspe Lorillard in *The Blind Bow-Boy,* had already established his defense: "How was it possible to read an author who never laughed? For it was only behind laughter that true tragedy could lie concealed, only the ironic author who could awaken the deeper emotions .... The only way to get the sense of this absurd, contradictory, and perverse existence into a book was to withdraw entirely from the reality."

The ability to accept the comic, to court amusement in facing the complications of social existence, was an antiphon to be sung over the insistent themes of tribulation. It was a way of living as well as a way of writing and could be neatly tuned to the fatalistic temper of the times. A lively sense of humor and absurdity, necessarily sophisticated at the intellectual level, was an invaluable antidote to the trials of the Twenties. These writers provided it. At a luncheon given by the Architectural League of Philadelphia—Van Vechten relates—he, Hergesheimer, and Cabell were guests of honor. At the conclusion of the program, a member addressing him as "Mr. Cabell" requested a signature in his copy of *Jurgen.* Van Vechten blithely complied with the request in a large flowing hand, and Cabell completed the fraud by signing the man's copy of *Peter Whiffle.* As an anecdote, the incident might be told of any novelist of the period, but except for these dealers in the arch phrase and the sophisticated whim it would be inconsistent with the personality and manner of their novels.

Art in a world of hard reality tends to become a servant rather than a master, an adjunct of utilitarian dreams rather than a goal for itself. The fiction of the Twenties, pessimistic and purposeful in its personal dramas and social protests, needed the balance of writers who could provide aesthetic, sophisticated, artful diversion concerned with manner as well as message. Imaginative fashioning, mature play of wit, and artifice, which was in the philosophy of J. K. Huysmans' perfect aesthete, Des Esseintes, "the distinctive mark of genius," are literary disciplines which would be sadly lacking in our fiction without the cameo charm of Elinor Wylie's dry-polished prose, Joseph Hergesheimer's well-furnished romances, painted as well as written, and James Branch Cabell's sly and and wry commentaries on life in Poictesme. One cannot dismiss Cabell as Oscar Cargill has in his discussion of these "exquisites" by labeling him "nothing more than our honest old friend Bill Arp, grown cynical and sophisticated," without revealing his real significance in an age that bred cynicism, sought sophistication, and lacked the finesse of style and grace in the arts. Neither can we dismiss the others merely because their artifice seems overcivilized in a period dominated by raw realists.

Van Vechten, of course, belongs with these artists, but his position rests on a number of innovations that call for separate consideration. His novels, as *Cue* magazine has said, "are, in a sense, a documentary study of the Twenties: clever, esoteric, thinly-veiled portraits of the period's leading bohemians." In this respect they move into the sphere of the novels of social consciousness, although the movement is characteristically light. In addition, they have in common with the novels of the personal intellectual quest the pursuit of a philosophy which could meet the demands of the age. Often vague and implicit, sometimes overt and insistent, it is a philosophy that curiously welds together modern fatalism with the limited operation of free will. Mabel Dodge Luhan has expressed, in what she recollects as her "only philosophy in those days," the fatalistic basis of this creed: "Let It happen. Let It decide. Let the great force behind the scenes direct the action. Have faith in life and do not hamper it or try to shape it." The last statement Van Vechten came to alter slightly. For him, as for much of his social milieu, *pattern* was a key word to life and art. Conventionally it might be conformity and regularity, but to him it was the antithesis. The object was to snatch pleasure wherever it could be found, and the individual not only could passively observe such patterns of pleasure, but could actively direct contrasting elements into amusing, diverting, and incongruous patterns.

For his novels, he selected the patterns of a number of popular subjects in contemporary fiction. *Peter Whiffle* capitalized on the post-war vogue of Continental settings. *The Tattooed Countess* fell in with the revolt from the village. *Nigger Heaven* celebrated the growing interest in Harlem life. *Spider Boy* lampooned Hollywood, a popular pastime in 1928. And *Parties* took stock of a decade which, at its conclusion, was given to looking on itself with a mixture of bewildered pride and grave misgivings. But each of these novels was singular within its type for the grotesque, ironic incongruities which served as the basis for both their diverting vitality and their thematic impact.

In his role of critic and essayist, Van Vechten brought a strange exotic flavor to literary taste in the United States, as well as giving his readers an indication of the eclectic background for his own fictions. Himself "guiltless of any ambition to be the great American novelist," he rarely commented on others who might demand similar titles.

> It is doubtless my limitation that the lesser figures in art have always succeeded in arousing my interest to a higher degree than the greater figures. I am quite willing to subscribe to the superior genius of Beethoven and Milton, but I prefer to listen to Scarlatti and to read the slighter works of Thomas Love Peacock. It is the odd, the charming, the glamorous, often the old-fashioned volume which has the compelling power with me.

Only partially an exception to this was his enthusiasm for the later work of Herman Melville in 1921, at which date other early Melville revivalists had discarded the works which followed *Moby Dick* as mysterious and tragic failures worth alluding to only as disappointing and anti-climactic addenda.

Van Vechten's other advocacies, most of which were collected in the volume smartly titled *Excavations,* fit the pattern more neatly. Edgar Saltus, that strange American aesthete dedicated to "style, style polished, style repolished" in the sensational pagan volumes which his wife reported were never written "less than three times," was the subject of one. Another celebrated the antique Philip Thicknesse, a spirited eighteenth-century adventurer who recorded his fabulous affairs with a charming frankness and dash. Most flamboyant of all the company, perhaps, was Ronald Firbank, the English eccentric with bird-of-paradise prose that crackled with electric sparks and confounded with bewildering indirection. Van Vechten single-handedly presided over the American introduction of this writer to a public in whose favor he is still growing. Others, appreciatively essayed, round out a perversely attractive assortment of forgotten or neglected stylists: the Continental Louise de la Ramée who wrote of romantic recklessness as Ouida; Henry Blake Fuller, the sympathetic cosmopolitan tragically tied to Chicago; the mystic Arthur Machen, who gained overdue recognition in consequence of his resurrection at the hands of Van Vechten; and the amazing M. P. Shiel, concocter of scientific fantasies and bold utopias. The list must be extended to many not included in *Excavations* to be complete, but these amply represent the peculiar flavor of Van Vechten's tastes in literature while indicating the discrimination which, except perhaps for the unguarded enthusiasm extended to Saltus, presided over his choices. They all had been, in one way or another, underrated or overlooked.

One more service as middleman between writer and public must be noted. In 1912 Van Vechten met Gertrude Stein in Paris. Miss Stein's companion, Alice B. Toklas, has recorded in brief the significance of this meeting. "It was on all sides love at first sight and the beginning of a long rare friendship, indescribable loyalty on his side, complete dependence on G. S.'s." Van Vechten has served practically as Gertrude Stein's agent ever since, and has borne much of the responsibility of getting her work before the public first and in their hearts afterward. As her literary executor, he has devoted himself since her death to the editing and complete presentation of her work.

Carl Van Vechten

5. BETWEEN 1915 AND 1932, when Van Vechten turned from the profession of writing to his highly successful career as a photographer, a total of nineteen volumes appeared under his name. Together with twenty-one prefaces and papers for other books, the editing of the cat tales in *Lords of the Housetops,* and frequent contributions to periodicals such as *The Smart Set, Vogue,* and *The Reviewer,* the list displays a prodigious literary output which is explained only partly by the fact that some of his volumes were compiled from essays first published separately. A considerable amount of editing and rewriting went into the preparation of these essays as they were being collected in book form. As his editorial experience increased, Van Vechten became more proficient as a prose stylist. The rather loose and extravagant rhetoric in some of his earlier work, written to meet the deadlines of the journals in which they appeared, became efficient, polished prose for publication in the more lasting print of a book. The editorial alterations made for successive appearances of a Van Vechten essay demonstrated his developing fastidiousness and taste in expression. In a letter to Van Vechten on December 30, 1924, James Branch Cabell, always a demanding critic of style, wrote of his pleasure with *Red,* Van Vechten's final collection of essays on music: "Your musical themes did not in this at all deter me, because I approached each paper, through a comparison with its earlier form, as an example of rewriting. . . . And all through, from my especial standpoint, I was applauding you. Your sentences become steadily more delightful."

Unlike Cabell and other authors whose books issue from a state of semi-seclusion, Van Vechten never let his writing interfere with the vigorous conviviality of his social existence. There was neither need nor desire for Van Vechten to retire—socially or geographically—to a personal Shangri-La where his writing could be done without interruption or distraction. The animated world of Van Vechten's books was the natural complement of the high life of Van Vechten's New York. The two were quite compatible and mutually necessary in his pattern of existence.

A summary of his activities can barely suggest the varied experience, friendships, and color, the hectic and strenuous living that Van

and the Twenties   23

Vechten crowded into the years between the First World War and the Great Depression. He became a fixture in the salon groups of Mabel Dodge, and his amazingly extensive association and friendship with all manner of celebrities, notables, and eccentrics both here and abroad could be matched by few of his contemporaries. After his marriage to the Russian actress, Fania Marinoff, he developed his own fabulous reputation as a genial, imaginative host drawing to the Van Vechten apartments the high and the low, the exotic and the plain, the dark and the light, the intellectual and the emotional representatives of literature, society, and the arts. All together, his social exploits qualify him as a ringmaster worthy of star billing in the Circus Maximus of the Twenties. And the resources of this gregarious commentator, whom so many of his contemporaries besides Emily Clark have "never ceased to consider one of the most diverting personalities in existence," extended from the main tent to the sideshows.

II. Music:

Criticism and Prophecy

FOR A COUNTRY which has a book of songs as the first volume printed on its shores, America has been tardy in bringing music to maturity in its national culture. Until the post-Civil War years, when the nation turned with sophomoric enthusiasm to cultural occasions and organizations, music, except in its folk traditions, was the rare luxury of the initiated few. By 1880, however, there was evidence that the American musician and his public intended to make up for lost time. The rising popularity of grand opera shifted the scene of musical activity gradually from Boston, long its American home, to New York. In the twenty years that closed the century, the list of musical organizations and occasions multiplied rapidly and widely, bringing music not only to the established society of the East Coast, but also to the burgeoning cultures which sent out their roots from Chicago, Cincinnati, and other growing centers of the Midwest.

1. IN THE OPENING DECADES of the twentieth century, America, having lately become familiar with three centuries of European music, rested easily for a while on that familiarity. The performers and the public combined to make music as much a commodity of culture as an aesthetic experience in art. The listener, aware in his limited experience only of popular themes from the masters, required the audition of nothing more to satisfy his musical taste. The performer, aware of this unimaginative satisfaction, catered to it, partly because he had to depend on the

AFTER PHOTOGRAPHING ETHEL WATERS IN "MAMBA'S DAUGHTERS"
CARL VAN VECHTEN PHOTOGRAPHED HIMSELF WITH HIS SUBJECT

support of his audience, and often because his own worship of the enshrined masters overbalanced any natural need he may have felt for novelty or variety. Such a situation was not stagnant, for the extended musical activity was still educating a nation in the art, but it was static, reducible in the business society of America to one more cultural item of stock in trade.

The popular conception of music, brought down to terms of the provincialism with which the Twenties were to break, was illustrated by the fate of German music during the First World War. Some symphony orchestras would play none. The Metropolitan Opera banned Wagner. Others yielded to public demand and de-emphasized the role of German compositions in their concerts, the taboo being extended to musicians with German names as well. A comparison of this with our conduct during World War II, when we continued to call hamburgers hamburgers and when we listened to Mendelssohn and Wagner without being tormented by delusions of subversion, indicates to some extent what we owe the forces of sophistication and sanity at work between the two wars. The music criticism of Carl Van Vechten is clearly one of these forces. Beginning in the years when musical America was content to let its engine die while gazing through the rear view mirror to admire what it had already seen, his essays directed attention to the road ahead. From the publication of his first collection in 1915, already talking of *Music After the Great War,* until the last volume, *Red* ("Red is the colour of youth. Oxen and turkeys are always enraged when they see it"[1]), in 1925, his writing urged that the art of music was in motion, and that the present and future tenses deserved a place in its discussion.

2. ANATOLE FRANCE spoke of criticism as the adventures of the soul among masterpieces. But criticism must deal with much art which does not, and perhaps is not meant to, qualify as a masterpiece.

1. The quotation, which serves as the book's inscription, is from Robert Schumann.

Often the personality and wit of the critic may be sufficient in themselves. These are the qualities which the critic must use to express himself and to reach others through the medium in which he works: literature. Criticism, despite academic dreams of objectivity, cannot be disembodied judgment, and the general reader should be thankful. As Peter Whiffle, speaking for his author, says, "We read the old critics to *find out about the critics,* not about the subjects on which they are writing. Consequently, it is only the critics who have been interesting personalities who are read through many generations."

The generalization may be a dangerous one to leave unqualified, but it holds more truth than error. The critic of any art cannot isolate his subject from either life or himself without narrowing the province of that art and diluting the strength of his own contribution to it. Paul Henry Lang has expressed the same thing in another way: "The true critic interprets life and its aims, and yet he speaks of music, books, or paintings as if they were the mere ornaments of life. It is this ironical circumstance which gives the great critics' writings that wisdom, humor, and force that is so strong that it must not be mentioned, for he who does not notice it will not discern the irony even if underscored." In content such a critic would command breadth of knowledge and experience; in manner he would present his own voice and personality, for the art and the life discussed in his writing are the art he knows and the life he observes. Among American music critics, James Gibbons Huneker, himself a model of the type, set the standards for this kind of critical writing.

There must be standards, but the two greatest are sympathy and its half-sister, sincerity. . . . The happy mean between swashbuckling criticism and the pompous academic attitude, dull but dignified, seems difficult of attainment. But it exists. To use the personal pronoun in criticism doesn't always mean "subjectivity." I don't believe in schools, movements, or schematologies, or any one method of seeing and writing. Be charitable, be broad—in a word, be cosmopolitan. He is a hobby of mine, this citizen of the world. A novelist may be provincial, parochial as the town pump, that is his picture; but a critic must not be narrow in his outlook on the world. He need not be so catholic as to admire both Cezanne and Cabanel, for they are mutually exclusive, but he should be cosmopolitan in his sympathies, else his standards are insufficient. The truth is, criticism is a full-sized man's job.

The precedent for such music criticism was not lacking in 1915. Huneker had been writing for years, and his audience was large. Oscar Thompson in *Practical Musical Criticism* reports that critical writings by Huneker had a following throughout the country never before granted to a New York critic. H. L. Mencken, in his essay on Huneker, remarks, "There is no stooping in his discourse; he frankly addresses himself to an audience that has gone through the forms, and so he avoids the tediousness of the ABC expositors. He is the only American musical critic, save Van Vechten, who thus assumes invariably that a musical audience exists." Lawrence Gilman's essays on modern music had also presented opinion and fact in the cosmopolitan tone of cultured conversation. In addition, the appearance of music essays as program notes for concerts gave impetus to this type of criticism, with Philip Hale's admirable work for the Boston Symphony setting the pace.

The animated style of Van Vechten's writing, together with his desire to broaden musical horizons in America, make him, if not a charter member of this new critical group, at least an illustrious and early initiate. He was perhaps more impudent, more wilfully shocking in his individuality, but his was the era of intellectual revolt against traditional standards. The license for his disregard of tradition came from a society finally ready to break with its provincial past. He opened fire on such established critics as H. T. Finck and Henry E. Krehbiel whenever he found them entrenched in the orderly confines of tradition. His frontal attack when defending Gustav Mahler's new instrumentation for certain masterworks against Krehbiel's charges of blasphemy for tampering with the classics is a memorable example. He attempted to remove the blinkers which had kept America's recognition of good music so limited and "safe." Through the appeal of his writing he attempted to share the breadth as well as the depth in music. What he wrote was vitally alive to him and remained alive in his prose. What he wrote of music was outspoken in opinion, but accurate in fact. Above all, it was a sincere and readable statement of its writer's own taste and personality. It ranged from a whimsical, jolly lampoon of contemporary American composers, utilizing quotations from a fugitive book which seriously catalogued small-town amateurs (obviously with an eye on sales to persons mentioned and their friends), to an impressive demonstration of first-hand knowledge, extensive research, thorough inquiry, and considered judgment brought to bear in an essay on the *Armide* of Gluck. If it often lacked what can be called "substance," the lack was purposeful, for it was meant to be read.

In the essay called "Why Music Is Unpopular," Van Vechten catalogued the sins of traditional music criticism and asserted his own creed. He indicted first the critics who fall upon quoting the poets to illustrate musical effects, and second those who feature academic sobriety and dry, pedantic purpose in their work. Such methods, he suggested, do more to harm music, by making it seem either precious or boring, than they do to help it. Music criticism could be both definitive (*The Music of Spain*) and provocative (the essays on interpreters, staging techniques, new composers, and the dance) in the writings of Van Vechten without sacrificing either writer or reader. His motive was simple and sensible: "Let more think about music; to make that possible curiosity must be stimulated, so that there may be a more general desire to *hear* music." His essays followed that aim.

In another respect, the criticism of Van Vechten followed the example of James Huneker. In its cosmopolitan outlook, it observed the correlation of the arts. As couriers of curiosity and culture, both found music the most beguiling of the arts, but they were unwilling to court her to the exclusion of her attractive sisters. Consistent with the true critic's need for breadth, they were at home with any aesthetic experience or artistic subject. Van Vechten, who according to Alfred Knopf "was always greatly concerned with the production of his books—in fact he designed most of them himself," brought his familiarity with literature, painting, dancing, and the theatre to bear on his discussion of music, and in many instances devoted whole essays to one or another of these interests. In addition, his taste for decoration, scene, color, and chiaroscuro consistently entered his essays. To most of America such freedom of reference was strange and suspect. "Persons who hear painting, see music, touch poems, taste symphonies, and write perfumes," said Huneker in comfortable self-defense, "are now classed by the psychical police as decadent, though such notions are as old as art and literature." Decadence somehow always has been a bad word in English.

With Van Vechten there was a more immediate basis for relating the arts: they were illustrative of elements inseparably inherent in music. "What most critics have forgotten is that in Music, matter, form, and idea are one," he declared. "In painting, in poetry, the idea, the words, the form, may be separated; each may play its part, but in music there is no idea without form, no form without idea." In another essay, "Variations on a Theme by Havelock Ellis," he approaches the relation of literature, painting, and music as media of expression. Ellis had suggested that painters were excellent writers, musicians poor. Although he mentions some significant exceptions, Van Vechten agrees; but he goes on to explain the importance to writers and painters of experience outside oneself, while the art of the musician need not be so encumbered. Conversely, words are an encumbrance to the musician, while to the painter and the writer, both accustomed to composing as an "eye," they are fluid and serviceable. The value of a working familiarity with the art of the painter and the writer for a critic of music is patent in this observation. In practice, it can be illustrated by the perception and feeling carried in a sentence from an essay on Waslav Nijinsky: "His dancing has the unbroken quality of music, the balance of great painting, the meaning of fine literature, and the emotion inherent in all these arts."

Van Vechten grew steadily more discursive throughout his career as a music critic, developing an easy, rambling, personal sort of discourse which disarms the seeker of more solid (or stolid) fare before it has the chance to discourage him. If his first volume had been a bit self-conscious and stiff (although not by ordinary standards), his second collection, *Music and Bad Manners*, assumed the familiar, anecdotal, whimsical style that was to remain in the ascendancy from then on. For all their diversity and even occasional perversity, however, the essays remained direct in their effects. Van Vechten ignored the customary half-protection of hedging. His convictions were never watered: "If every time I expressed a personal feeling (and all my feelings and tastes are intensely personal) I followed with something like this, 'it seems to me,' or 'this may or may not be true,' or 'according to my taste,' or 'Mr. Thing does not agree with me,' my utterances would lose whatever force or charm they possess and they would be so clogged with extraneous qualifications that no one would read them." This is the explanation of his reputation for brashness and impetuous whim. The basic formula for his critical judgment he declared even more simply: "Imitative work is always bad. Music that tries to be something that something else has been may be thrown aside as worthless."

3. *FROM THE EIGHTIES ON*, opera flourished in New York and in America. It had been a noteworthy part of America's musical activity through much of the nineteenth century, but in the first two decades of the present century opera fed the public's appetite for glamor and celebrity as well as for artistic entertainment. Commercial radio was not yet born, and motion pictures were in their awkward childhood; opera and opera stars provided the entertainment and glitter that these mass media were soon to usurp. The stars of opera were familiar to all classes, from the sophisticated devotee to the adolescent of the hinterlands who never expected to attend a performance. This broad appeal and the social importance attached to the patronage of opera assured its popularity and support, but at the same time allowed producers and performers to concentrate their efforts on providing glamor and social occasions to the general neglect of artistic improvement. As a result, the audience was on hand, but it displayed no taste; impresarios and producers had only to present opera and opera stars to satisfy their paying public. If the performers were sufficiently colorful and the occasion sufficiently patronized by the cultured and elite, little else was required.

The task of the critic under these circumstances was to applaud whatever excellence could be found in opera and to encourage innovations and imagination which would make the offerings even more satisfying as both art and entertainment, for, to some extent, the producers of opera as well as the audience had to be educated. To Van Vechten the solution was plain: whatever had life, personality, and artistic imagination was good; whatever lacked these qualities was poor. He found the interpreters, the performing stars, chiefly in the first category, the unimaginative stage productions through which they moved in the second. He welcomed the change in the emphasis of the singer from *bel canto,* the flamboyant perfection of vocal tone and technique, to expressive, interpretive singing consistent with the dramatic role. "The new art of the singer," he wrote in the essay of that name, "should develop to the highest degree the significance of the text." He could cite Mary Garden in this respect as the most able exponent. His volume of essays devoted to interpreters and interpretations admiringly evoked the art of such singing actors and actresses as Feodor Chaliapin, Olive Fremstad, Mariette Mazarin, Geraldine Farrar, and Miss Garden, fully appreciating the personality each carried into an operatic role, while recognizing the shortcomings, mostly musical but sometimes dramatic, which stood between performance and perfection.

Van Vechten was aware of the ephemeral nature of a performer's interpretation. Traditionally, it was placed in the province of journalists who recorded the day to day events in music, being too short-lived to endure the demands of critical longevity faced by the author of books about music; but to Van Vechten it was worthy of perpetuation. For this reason *Interpreters and Interpretations* is almost unique in our literature on the arts. Only one other volume, Henry T. Parker's 1922 collection of essays, *Eighth Notes,* shares its concern with the lasting contributions of performers, and this work, culled from the author's columns for the *Boston Evening Transcript,* is much the more temporal and superficial of the two. Van Vechten succeeded in revealing the personality of great interpretive art. His desire for the dramatic fulfillment of an operatic role demanded a deeper satisfaction than operatic music alone could provide.

When he found a performer who believed in hyphenating the presentation as well as the name of music-drama, his gratitude for the pleasure that performer gave him was expressed in a prose dedicated to capturing the experience itself. Although his essay on Geraldine Farrar was tempered by reservations not present in his tributes to Olive Fremstad and Mary Garden, Van Vechten must have been pleased to report her expression of her art to him: "In my humble way I am an actress who happens to be in opera. I sacrifice tonal beauty to dramatic fitness every time I think it is necessary for an effect, and I shall continue to do it. I leave mere singing to the warblers. I am more interested in acting myself." The flippant disregard for music in such a statement, Van Vechten implied, was indicative of Miss Farrar's peculiar failings, but her defiance of stifling tradition was the mark of her success.[2] This sincere appreciation of the personal force lent to art by its interpreter never left Van Vechten. Again, in 1947, in the program notes written for a recital by Marian Anderson on June 27 of that year, he expressed his familiar pleasure in the creative immersion of an interpreter in her art: "What I noticed more than anything else about her was a kind of dedication of spirit."

The performers, therefore, were doing their part to supply vitality and artistic imagination. What needed more attention in American opera was the style and technique of the stage production. He found it static, unimaginative, and oppressive. The life of the music and the interpreter often was smothered by the pomposity and dullness of the complete presentation. There was "no reason why it should be so solemnly conducted," he complained. "There are times at the Metropolitan Opera House when one expects to hear the gong of high mass sound or Professor William Lyon Phelps lecturing on Browning." He saw no reason why the company that scheduled performances at the Metropolitan should not offer Gilbert and Sullivan operas, particularly *The Mikado,* which he referred to as "probably the best opera ever written to an English book." He criticized

2. Van Vechten began his essay on Geraldine Farrar with his disappointment that her autobiography was so inferior to the personality and life of her art. His review of Mary Garden's autobiography in *The Saturday Review of Literature* for May 26, 1951, expresses the same regret.

the lack of art and imagination in staging, casting, setting, and other technical elements of production. In an essay of June, 1914, he heralded the future use of suggestive, artistically functional stage settings to replace the customary flatness of conventional drapes and realistic, photographic accuracy, citing the theories of the little known Gordon Craig and the work of the Russian Ballet to indicate the trend. A year later he traced the theories of Craig back to the work of Adolphe Appia, who served as a fountainhead for modern staging technique, much as Stanislavsky was the revolutionary theorist for acting. In Appia's theories and plans for staging Wagner was the basis for the functional, artistic methods later used by Craig, Robert Edmond Jones, and others who set out to revolutionize stage decoration, lighting, and effects. We have since seen the fulfillment of their ideas in the innovations of Rudolph Bing at the Metropolitan. Van Vechten pointed to these methods as a means of fulfilling the need created by the lack of taste and artistry given to the staging of opera—particularly that of Wagner. Reminding his reader of the Wagnerian ideal "in which the picture, the word, and the tone shall all be a part of the drama," he envisioned its realization, adding as his characteristic comment that art was not static, that outmoded tradition must give way to the imaginative improvements of time. "Wagner invented a new form of stage art but only in a small measure did he succeed in perfecting a method for its successful presentation." To cling to the "traditions" of Bayreuth in 1915 was as vain as to insist on preferring gaslight to electric incandescence.

4. *"MUSIC FOR MUSEUMS?"* written in January, 1915, announced Van Vechten's objections to the standard repertoire of symphony concerts in America; the orchestras improved in musicianship and finesse, he granted, but they played the same established music so continually that it paled from excessive repetition and familiarity. This was one reason for his extensive treatment of new, experimental composers. The other was his sincere belief in the merit of their work and the musical future their revolutionary methods promised. In his first volume he

declared that traditional harmony had been exhausted in its conventions, and that the pursuit of disharmony would direct music in the future. The complaint against contemporary composers, he pointed out, has always been that they could not write melody and that they broke "rules" in their harmony. Surveying the musical scene of June, 1915, he concluded that the world would look to Igor Stravinsky, Arnold Schoenberg, and, to a lesser degree, the young Erich Korngold for "messages in tone, disharmonic by nature, and with a complexity of rhythm so complex that it became simple."

To strengthen his plea for recognition and performance of the new, prophetic music, he marshaled whatever comment he could find in others who shared his view, but America provided little help. Europeans he could quote much more freely and to the point. He selected as his keynote the pertinent remarks of Arnold Schoenberg in his *Handbuch der Harmonielehre:*

> If anyone feels dissatisfied with his time, let it not be because that time is no longer the good old time, but because it is not yet the new and better time, the future.
>
> Though I refrain from overprizing originality, I cannot help valuing novelty and the unknown; and therefore, not without excuse, we often hold what is novel to be identical with what is good and beautiful.

Later, he reproduced for the same purpose, a conversation with Feodor Chaliapin in which the Russian singer complains of a stodgy American audience "content to listen forever to *Faust* and *Lucia.*"

> In Europe it is different. There you will find the desire for novelty in the theatre. There is a keen interest in the production of a new work. It is all right to enjoy the old things, but one should see life. The audience at the Metropolitan Opera House reminds me of a family that lives in the country and won't travel. It is satisfied with the same view of the same garden forever.

Van Vechten's most direct and concerted defense of the new music is found in "The Bridge Burners," from the 1916 volume *Music and Bad Manners*. This essay utilizes comment from many an authoritative voice and categorically upholds the artistic fidelity of such controversial composers as Stravinsky, Schoenberg, and Leo Ornstein. Elsewhere, he gave them individual attention.

His most enthusiastic regard was given to the exciting music of Igor Stravinsky, of whom Van Vechten was the first American to write at any length with enthusiasm, authority, prophecy, and insight. "Igor Stravinsky: a New Composer," dated August 6, 1915, discusses all the works of the Russian to that time, including sections devoted to *Petrouchka* (1911), *The Rites of Spring* (1913—this selection was so new that its English title had not been established; Van Vechten refers to it as "The Sacrifice to the Spring"), and *The Nightingale* (1914). Van Vechten had heard and marveled at performances of these works in Paris and London; America, as yet, had heard little of, and knew less about, their creator. Six months later another essay on Stravinsky, "A New Principle in Music" dealt with the singular instrumentation featured in *Petrouchka* and succeeding works, and the composer's utilization of folk music and popular songs as functional parts of his compositions. "It would not surprise me at all to discover *Hello Frisco* bobbing up in one of his future works," the critic wrote, calling once again on a blithe clairvoyance to predict Stravinsky's use of American popular music and jazz.

Another little known artist discussed by Van Vechten with special pleasure was the obscure, capricious but influential figure in the French musical renaissance, Erik Satie. The novelty, the whimsy, the disarming simplicity of Satie's sketches, together with their place in *fin de siècle* Paris and French impressionism in the arts, gave this curious initiator an affectionate place in Van Vechten's collection of iconoclasts. "Timorous, meticulous, mincing, neat, petulant, petty, are some of the adjectives one might apply to this music, and yet none of them exactly describes its effect, half-spiritual, half-mocking! Is there any other music like it?" he asked. The answer had to be negative, but James Huneker qualified it with praise for the essay, derision for its subject:

Carl Van Vechten has told us of Erich [sic] Satie ... who sets snails and oysters to music, and, no doubt, has composed a Cootie's Serenade for wind instruments with a fine-tooth comb obbligato, and we are amazed at the critical exposition of such a perplexing "case." To let his music speak for itself, would be unwise, as it is not sufficiently explicative .... After Van Vechten has polished off his man, we feel that we know all about Satie, so much so that we never wish to hear a bar of his crustacean music. The difference between tweedle-dum and tweedle-dee is infinitesimal, but that very difference may contain great art.

It is amusing to find Huneker giving Van Vechten the same sort of wry treatment the latter had so often given others, but in this instance the older Huneker had read neither wisely nor well. The essay in question made no pretense of introducing "great music," but offered novel, interesting, and historically significant art. And Huneker would have had trouble finding "a bar of his crustacean music" even if he did decide to hear it. As the essay clearly pointed out, Satie had freed himself from "the tyranny of the bar line," and had composed and published his curious music without any.

It was Van Vechten's purpose in discussing the strange methods of these innovators to excite enough interest to assure a demand that they be heard. While he wrote competently of their techniques and effects, he wrote also to make their names and the personality of their music familiar to the American musician and listener. To this end (and no doubt to gratify his own taste for novelty and striking contrast) he appended to *The Merry-Go-Round* "An Impertinent Catalogue" of epithets which he titled "The Modern Composer at a Glance." While the list displays Van Vechten in his most whimsical and trivial dress, some of the descriptions are apt enough in revealing both their critic and the composers to deserve repetition:

Arnold Schoenberg: Six times six is thirty-six—and six is ninety-two!

Erik Satie: A mandarin with a toy pistol firing into a wedding cake.

Giacomo Puccini: Pinocchio in a passion.

Paul Dukas: A giant eating bonbons.

Claude Debussy: Chantecler crows *pianissimo* in whole tones.

Richard Strauss: An ostrich *not* hiding his head.

Percy Grainger: An effete Australian chewing tobacco.

Edward Elgar: The footman leaves his accordion in the bishop's carriage.

Igor Stravinsky: Paul Revere in Russia.

Engelbert Humperdinck: His master's voice.

In all Van Vechten's essays about the moderns and the future moderns, his mission is given a personal touch. He had found their new vitality exciting and remarkable; others might, too. He was careful to attempt only to say why *he* liked modern music. "If I were to tell others how to like it," he said, "I should be forced to resort to a single sentence: 'Open your ears.'"

He might have added "the mind's eye" to this advice, for there was in his essays, as in the music of his favorites, the possibility of secondary experience, the awakening of emotion and association through the musical suggestion of aesthetic imagery. His first book had defiantly demonstrated his preference for the emotional response to impressionism over the austere intellectualism of musical mathematics. "Chamber music!" he had blasphemed. "Its title explains it. It is music intended to be played at home ... *music intended to be played,* not to be listened to, except, perhaps, by some doting members of the performers' families." In his second volume, more mature in its manner and rhetoric, he expressed his interest in the rise of program music, observing that "while painting has become less and less an attempt to represent nature, music has more and more attempted concrete representation." The traditional forces that opposed such sympathies and dismissed such music were formidable. Daniel Gregory Mason was condemning Strauss for his childish "programmism," Debussy for his "sensationalism," both typical to the traditional critic of the new music which, he asserted, pandered to the elements in music which were not the music itself. "Programmism," in Mason's view, afforded stories and realistic sounds; and impressionism, or "sensationalism," feeding on novelty, substituted harmonic experiments for lofty melody, aiming "primarily at sensuous rather than mental or spiritual values." While such an opinion can still be respected as the expression of a cultivated, intellectual taste, its lack of foresight is amply demonstrated by the trends of music in our century.

5. *CARL VAN VECHTEN'S* most distinct contribution to our literature on music is his proficient volume, *The Music of Spain* (1918). "Music and Spain," an exploratory essay printed earlier in *The Merry-Go-Round,* was meant to fill a surprising gap in our musical knowledge, for no previous general commentary on its subject had appeared in our language.[3] Around this center, Van Vechten's interest in the lively arts of the Spanish and his assiduous search through its backgrounds and manifestations built a compendium of Spanish music which still serves both scholarly and curious readers as an absorbing, although unconventional study of its subject. The central essay, which explored such varied commentaries as Richard Ford's *Gatherings From Spain,* Gautier's *Voyage en Espagne,* and Havelock Ellis's *The Soul of Spain* for its first-hand anecdotes and observations, is a thorough study of the forms and spirit of Spanish dances, the music, and the musicians of Spain. As published later in *The Music of Spain,* the study includes forty-eight pages of notes on the text which expand the original essay and document the comprehensive research supporting the work. In this separate volume Van Vechten appended a *"histoire sommaire de Carmen"* entitled "From George Borrow to Mary Garden," which traces *Carmen* from the sources used by Prosper Mérimée through Bizet's operatic adaptation, adding a catalogue

3. Although its approach to the subject was quite different, *Histoire de la Musique: Espagne,* by A. Soubies was published in Paris in 1900, eighteen years before Van Vechten's study appeared.

of performances which culminates in Miss Garden's interpretation. *Carmen* is mentioned only briefly in the central study, "Music and Spain," because, as the essay demonstrates, it is not really Spanish. "The Land of Joy," a record of Van Vechten's overflow of emotional and artistic satisfaction after his first encounter with authentic Spanish dancing and singing, is also included in the volume. The occasion it celebrated was the otherwise unheralded New York performance of "The Land of Joy" by a Spanish company in 1917. Elsewhere, he rounded out his excursions into Iberian arts by reporting the activities in cosmopolitan New York of the Spanish theatre, and by devoting an informative, appreciative essay to the leading representative of the modern school of Spanish composition, Isaac Albéniz, both appearing in his next book, *In the Garret*.

6. *THE SPIRITED ZARZUELAS,* fandangos, and jotas of Spain were not the only dances that supplied subjects for Van Vechten's criticism. He wrote dance reviews for the *New York Times* and published essays covering the field of the dance from early ballet to Isadora Duncan. Excited by the accomplishments of modern ballet, he wrote favorably of Leo Delibes, naming him "the father of the modern ballet" because his ballet music was the first to give the dancer something deeply expressive; before Delibes, musical scores had been shallow and mechanical, composed chiefly to show off technique.

He wrote intimately and skilfully of the Russian Ballet as early as November, 1915, praising in detail its technical and emotional union of many arts: painting, music, drama, design, poetry, and staging. He continually called the attention of operatic producers to the example of artistic unity he found in this ballet, for it provided the aesthetic taste and over-all effects that opera lacked. The new art of stage decoration he found already an integrated part of the Russian dancers' productions.

He singled out the unbelievable artistry of Waslav Nijinsky for the most thoroughly encomiastic of all his discussions of interpretive art.

The essay, one of his most brilliant and lucid pieces of writing, happily avoided treating the spectacular aspects of Nijinsky's dancing as such. Instead, the author's wonder and praise were given to the consummate wholeness of the performance, the flawless expression of the dancer's complete interpretation in every nuance of movement, as well as in the strenuous display of agility. "It seems to me," he wrote as he considered Nijinsky's achievement, "that in his chosen medium he approaches perfection. What he attempts to do, he always does perfectly. Can one say as much for any other interpreter?"

His essay on the interpretive dance techniques of Isadora Duncan had only a spark of the enthusiastic fire found in his tribute to the Russian. It did, however, recognize a revolutionary spirit in this forerunner of modern dance, and it celebrated in her work two of the qualities which he demanded of the interpretive artist, devoted spirit and unique personality.

The earlier dance reviews which Van Vechten wrote for the *New York Times* were printed unsigned, but many of them were revived for publication by *Dance Index* in its three-in-one issue for September, October, and November of 1942. The quality and significance of this work, even at this late date, inspired John Martin's tribute to the collection:

> [These reviews] form a body of criticism that is an uncommonly valuable contribution to America's literature in that field. Though they were written thirty years ago, their judgments are as sound as they ever were and the prescience they exhibit in an art in which America ... was abysmally illiterate bespeaks a remarkably sensitive and forward-looking mind. That they played a major part in the creation of public taste cannot be gainsaid.

It is noteworthy to report that by 1946, in his review of Grace Robert's *Borzoi Book of Ballets,* Van Vechten was able to write, with his customary appreciation for the gifted interpreter, of Jerome Robbins, Agnes DeMille, Nora Kaye, and other successful American artists in the field of ballet.

7. UNTIL THE FIRST WORLD WAR, American music had not been productive, it had been imitative. It assimilated much but contributed little. Our nineteenth-century composers and those who carried American composition into the twentieth century wrote music in America, not American music. The notable exception was Stephen Foster.

The source, the color, and the native appeal of Foster's songs came from the unstudied melodic style and rhythm of the music developed by the American Negro. These songs reflected the upper and lower surfaces of a folk personality—gaiety and resignation, an abandonment to present joy and a timeless, rootless nostalgia: the minstrel and the mourner. These dual elements spread through twentieth-century American music as jazz, a homogenized term for the split personality shown in the spontaneous combustion of "dixieland" improvisation and the fluid lament of the blues.

Writing for the generation of the Twenties, Van Vechten was one of a very few who recognized in jazz music and ragtime, the middle ground between jazz and its folk origins, an indigenous art capable of giving blood and tissue to the musical bones imported from Europe. In the early Twenties, American jazz had invaded Paris, and that city's reception of it included a flood of serious essays by Parisian intellectuals. In 1924, Gilbert Seldes still courted derision by writing, "If—before we have produced something better—we give up jazz we shall be sacrificing nearly all there is of gaiety and liveliness and rhythmic power in our lives." In an essay dated January 23, 1917, Van Vechten approved and applauded the popular work of such ragtime composers as Lewis F. Muir, Irving Berlin, and Louis A. Hirsch, "the true grandfathers of the Great American Composer of the year 2001." On their popular (hence traditionally to be regarded as inferior) product, he pronounced prophetic judgment: "It is the only music produced in America today which is worth the paper it is written on. It is the only American music which is enjoyed by the nation . . . ; it is the only American music which is heard abroad . . . , and it is the only music on which the musicians of our land can build . . . in the future."

Carl Van Vechten

To the bulk of his contemporary critics, a confusion of the art with the lack of intellectual austerity involved in its production rendered jazz insignificant, if not profane. To the traditional critic like Daniel Gregory Mason it was "a meaningless stir-about, a commotion without purpose, an epilepsy simulating controlled muscular action." Mason took supercilious issue with Van Vechten, disparaging the latter's remarks concerning the potential variety in the syncopation of ragtime. He scoffed at those who "have even challenged comparison of it with the rhythmic vigors of Beethoven and Schumann," and footnoted this, "See, for instance, Mr. Carl Van Vechten's 'Interpreters and Interpretations.'" The tremendous variety in modern jazz syncopation certainly fulfills Van Vechten's expectations. His remarks in that book have been echoed in the scholarly prose of an objective authority, Adolfo Salazar, who wrote in 1946 that American jazz "undoubtedly awakens stimuli in the composer, for example for its combinations of time values and its superimpositions of rhythms on a constant monorhythmic base with its one beat which permits, obviously, of every variety of superimposed polyrhythms."

What set Van Vechten apart from other serious critics writing early treatments of jazz was his predilection for animation and personality in art, and his instinctive rapport with its sources. He listened to jazz because it was alive, because it was emotionally expressive, not because he was a music critic covering a beat. His enthusiasm was primary—the result of personal pleasure; his critical appraisal was the formal contemplation of the thing that stimulated that pleasure.

His active participation in the recognition of the Negro's music was one of the first bold steps in a life which has since contributed so much to the acceptance of that race's accomplishments. He was the logical writer to introduce, through the pages of *Vanity Fair* and other publications, Ethel Waters (who has remembered him graciously in her autobiography) and the unrelated queens of the blues, Clara, Mamie, and Bessie Smith. Reminiscing of the latter, now firmly established in the hierarchy by the serious historians of jazz, Van Vechten remembers having "boxes and boxes" of her phonograph records "which I played and played in the early 'twenties and everybody who came to my apartment was invited to hear them." W. C. Handy, the hardy composer of the *St. Louis Blues,* after citing the support of the blues by the Negro publications *Opportunity* and *The Crisis,* wrote: "But more than any other, perhaps, the pen that set tongues to wagging, ears listening and feet dancing to the blues was that of the celebrated author and writer, Carl Van Vechten, who said the folk blues 'far transcend the spirituals in their poetic values, while as music they are frequently of at least equal importance.' "

The difference was that Van Vechten not only thought about the Negro's music and wrote of it, he felt it and understood it. He had lived close to it for ten years when he wrote in his valedictory to music criticism in March, 1924, "Jazz may not be the last hope of American music, nor yet the best hope, but at present, I am convinced, it is its only hope."

8. *ONE OF THE MOST REMARKABLE THINGS* about music in twentieth-century America is its ubiquity. Through our media of mass entertainment, music reaches us publicly and privately more insistently and in more variety than any other of the fine arts. It confronts all levels of America through radio, the movies, television, the theatre, the dance orchestras, the jazz bands, phonograph recordings, the concert hall, school bands and orchestras, and the omnipresent juke box accepting coins for three-minute serenades in every corner of the country.

There is scarcely any organized entertainment in America that does not involve music. The unseen musician at the electronic organ serves radio drama much as the indefatigable movie house pianist served the early films. Clubs, restaurants, taverns, and hamburger kiosks each feature appropriate musical background as a part of the pleasure and atmosphere of dining out, ranging from the suave dinner music of an ensemble in sophisticated attire, to the offerings of remote control record selectors which confront every patron of the drinks-and-eats establishment. Even the masculine haven of athletic sports has taken in music as a featured partner. Football games vie for attention with the snappy productions of costumed bands monopolizing time-out periods and entertainment between the halves. Baseball parks fill the intervals between innings with recorded music played over their public address systems and for special games provide bands to enliven the occasion. The importance of a sporting event is signalled by the presence of a famous singer leading the national anthem.

As critics and citizens we may resent some of the musical activities in our society; singing commercials on the radio and the amplified programs of music that meet us whether we are willing or not in such public places as New York's Grand Central Station have their insidious aspects. Yet, it would be difficult to deny that the musical quotient of the average American and the vitality of American music have benefited enormously from the wholesale distribution of music in the United States.

The increase in the occasions for music has been equalized by a greater variety of music produced. Musicians as well as non-musicians have become familiar with the whole range of American music. The arrangers for popular bands and experimental jazz units have gradually reached out for the fullness and technical effects of serious music, while their own innovations in harmony and rhythm have been caught and reflected by serious composers. Studio orchestras, performing for radio, movies, and recordings, have enlisted the talents of some of the nation's most skilled performers, and have featured stylish arrangements which fill in the narrowing middle ground between popular and serious music. Through such diversification, "popular" music has become serious, and "serious" music has become popular.

In addition, music has become an artistic supplement to drama. Its powers of suggestion, association, color, and mood have made it an invaluable asset to emotional effects in any field. Radio would be pale indeed without music. The motion pictures engage distinguished composers to write musical scores appropriate to the demands of films. Musical comedy on the stage produces music which is less and less ephemeral as it becomes more and more integrated with the stage production.

At the outset of the Twenties, ragtime, jazz, tin-pan alley, Broadway musicals, effervescent vaudeville, and musical accompaniment for the silent movies—all the vital beginnings—awaited only the perfection of the phonograph, the rise of commercial radio, and the maturity of film techniques. Carl Van Vechten was virtually the only critic of his era who detected the vitality and promise of these elements and wrote prophetically of their place in American music.

In 1915, when silent movies were still a national novelty, Van Vechten saw the need for expressive music in the new art medium. This music, he predicted with excitement, would not be retarded by the traditional millstones of "working-out" or over-all development, and would be more demanding of the futurist composer. "The ultimate moving picture score," he wrote, "will be something more than sentimental accompaniment," observing that the task would be worthy of the greatest musical talent. "For the same reason that d'Annunzio, very early in the career of the moving picture, wrote a scenario for a film, I should not be surprised to learn that Richard Strauss was under contract to construct an accompaniment to a screened drama." The prediction that sounded so glib in 1915 has been amply validated since by the movie music of such composers as Aaron Copland, Kurt Weil, Serge Prokofiev, Dmitri Shostakovitch and Virgil Thomson.

In the same essay, Van Vechten deplored the rehash of stereotyped selections and themes used by the movie house orchestras as a patchwork score to accompany silent films. "It is strange," he lamented, "but it has occurred to no one that the moving picture demands a *new* kind of music." The readers of this essay, if one can accept the response of Russell Ramsey in his review as typical, treated "Music for the Movies" as a thought which "excites [Van Vechten's] irrepressible humor," and accepted it as the amusing fantasy of a whimsical writer.

In "The Importance of Electrical Picture Concerts," he played with the idea that the incidental music and intermission concerts at moving picture theatres in 1916 were becoming important for the audition of seldom concertized compositions. In the variety they sought, Americans were finally breaking away from the closed shop of concert favorites, and many members of the audiences who heard these performances were gaining an accelerated musical education. Those who heard music only in the theatres were being initiated painlessly, while those limited by what they heard in the traditional concert were developing taste and knowledge.

He extended these ideas in a 1921 essay, "Music for Program Notes," to suggest a union of the concert and the movies. This essay discussed the projection of pictorial as well as printed program notes, and proposed that someone "illustrate symphonic poems, all program music, indeed, by appropriate accompanying action on the screen." Van Vechten chose Dukas' "The Sorcerer's Apprentice" as an example of program music which could utilize visual action to match the music. He cited in detail the theme of the broomstick demon, visualizing the scene-with-music, and concluded: "This magic broom, pouring out pails of water, could be cleverly counterfeited on the silver sheets, and, I think that the music performed before this appropriate action would make treble the ordinary effect."

In 1940 *Fantasia*, the joint achievement of Leopold Stokowsky and Walt Disney, brought the American public a combination of the concert and the movies that was strikingly similar to the union Van Vechten had envisaged in 1921. With a newly developed sound system reproducing the concert orchestra, the Disney film presented animated drawings to illustrate symphonic compositions. And one of the selections, featuring Mickey Mouse at the mercy of the magic broom and its pails of water, was "The Sorcerer's Apprentice."

The curious similarity was coincidental. When it was called to his attention, Gunther R. Lessing, vice-president of Walt Disney Productions, found after consulting Disney and others concerned with their enterprise that the Van Vechten essay had no direct connection with either the conception or the production of *Fantasia*. For some ten years before his work on this film, Disney had been producing short subjects under the generic title "Silly Symphony," the action of which was descriptive of well-known musical compositions. The choice of "The Sorcerer's Apprentice" was as natural to Disney, evidently, as it had been to Van Vechten. But the 1921 essay made no mention of a personable mouse as the apprentice: Van Vechten's concern was to have the movie enhance the effect of the music.

Besides his active support of the Negro's music, Van Vechten celebrated the contributions of popular music-hall performers to American art and entertainment. During his younger days in Cedar Rapids, he had maintained an enthusiasm for the personalities of this theatrical realm. In New York he sensed its part in the growing musical expression of America. In "Old Days and New," he discussed the popular appeal of the stage musical with sentiment and critical praise, calling forth in April, 1917, a parade of contemporary celebrities such as Al Jolson, Elsie Janis, Jerome Kern, Fanny Brice, and Irving Berlin, the majority of whom are still familiar to and beloved by the American public. Van Vechten's regard for the songs of Irving Berlin was especially aggressive. In January, 1918, he wrote, "Personally I can say that I prefer Irving Berlin's music to that of Edward MacDowell and I would like to have some one prove to me that this position is untenable." In the verve and personality of all the music-hall artists he recognized a lively partner for American jazz.

Van Vechten's final book of essays on musical subjects reflected a personal distaste for the artificial occasions for hearing music. Through his career as a critic he had attended concert after concert with a growing resentment at the necessity of hearing other people's programs in the harsh, unsuitable, over-lighted public surroundings of the concert hall. The two essays which conclude the volume, "On Hearing What You Want When You Want It" (1920), and "Cordite for Concerts" (1921), are a fitting climax to a career which had foreseen so much of America's musical development. The first of these, the title of which was so perfect for latter day advertising of phonograph records, bewailed the fact that music occupies time rather than space, and, for that reason, places the listener at the mercy of the selection of others. No other art, he pointed out, established such a discouraging condition for its audience; music needed to become more individually accessible, subject to personal taste and mood, before it could fulfill its artistic role completely.

"Cordite for Concerts" complained of the uncomfortable and inappropriate settings one had to endure in order to hear music. Its personal revolt was as straightforward and indignant as anything its congenial

Carl Van Vechten

author had written: ". . . concerts should not be given in halls . . . , even the idea of the concert as it exists is a false and artificial conception. It is impossible for me to enjoy music in a brilliantly lighted, badly ventilated auditorium."

Today we are seldom aware that such battles had to be fought. We relax in our living rooms to hear the music we choose from our record libraries, or we listen in the same position of ease to the brilliant broadcasts of our great symphonies. Frank Lloyd Wright works over his architectural drawing board in his studio or moves through the rambling buildings at Taliesen with hidden speakers offering the accompaniment of Mozart and Bach. The factory worker and the garage mechanic perform their tasks against the background of recorded music broadcast for their pleasure and efficiency during the working day; the midnight shift has the company of an all-night record show on its radio to provide companionship and music for its lonely hours. Jazz has become the subject of concerts, and concert music has invaded the people's arena. The visions of music being both artistic and popular, active in our environment as both a social and personal pleasure at all levels of society, have been fulfilled.

9. *WITH THE PUBLICATION* of *Red* in 1924, Van Vechten announced his voluntary retirement as a music critic. He was forty-four, and for about six years had held doubts about continuing this role. In his youth, he recalled, he had held the conviction that age was a mark of the doldrums, that old dogs ignored new tricks. "When I was younger I held the firm belief that after forty the cells hardened and that prejudices were formed which precluded the possibility of the welcoming of novelty. From almost the moment I began to write on the subject of music, therefore, I took it upon myself to attack the older men who had closed their minds to new ideas." After the years devoted to concerts and causes, he added with a typical humorous irony, "I recognized the symptoms of age creeping upon me. I began to prefer Johann Strauss waltzes to the last sonatas of Beethoven; Chopin pleased me more than Brahms."

He may have recalled, whimsically, a passage in praise of Stravinsky's originality written eight years earlier, in which he had mused, parenthetically,

> You must realize how much your mind wanders at a symphony concert. It is impossible to concentrate one's complete attention on the performance of a long work except at those times when some new phrase or some new turn in the working-out of a theme strikes the ear. There is so much of the music that is familiar, because it has occurred in so much music before.... There are those, I am forced to admit, who can only concentrate on that which is perfectly familiar to them.

Looking back on his earliest attempts at "review-criticism," James Huneker wrote: "I saved these notices and I find that they read like the regulation bone-dry critique, with its spilth of adjectives and its amateurish omniscience. I had horse sense enough to avoid too many technical terms, and the criticisms that read the most reasonable are those in which the news element predominates. But the critical values! Oh!" Van Vechten expressed a similar distaste for his own early work, seen in retrospect, by footnoting a reference to "Music for Museums?" as "the only section I can recall with any patience of a vile book (my first), Music After the Great War." In 1924, however, as he granted permission to a younger generation of critics "to transfer what I said ten years ago about Stravinsky and Satie to Darius Milhaud and the young Italians," there was more reason to agree with Ernest Newman's third-person review of his own career as a music critic: "It is, of course, some consolation to him to run over mentally the record of his colleagues and to recognize how much more of error they have talked than he, and how much less of truth."

III. LITERATURE:

Exquisite and Rowdy

TO APPEAR SOPHISTICATED one may consult a sampling of the world's literature and art, and thus construct an eclectic personality to wear, like a fashionable suit of clothes dressing a wooden mannequin. The ultimate sophisticate, however, displays a consistent personality which provides the appetite, directs the exploration, and assimilates its experiences as a real expression of itself. The reader meets this genuine sophistication in Carl Van Vechten.

In his essays one is invited to share the appetite, the exploration, and the discoveries. In his novels one meets the personality itself, extemporizing variations on the themes of its experience. Through them all appear the inferences and allusions of a writer secure in his background and taste, generously conceding to his reader a breadth and sophistication commensurate with his own. This is a considerable concession, since the random allusions and suggestions appear in what Hunter Stagg has called "journeys among things that can dwell only in the memories of a man who has known almost every interesting person from Hollywood to Buda Pesth, and done nearly everything from attempting to collect 'The Folk Songs of Iowa' to discoursing upon fowls on the terrace of Windsor Castle and acting in the moving pictures in Nassau."

1. IT IS SIGNIFICANT that Van Vechten sparkles when he refers to the Eighteen-Eighties in Paris, for from his familiarity with the achievements of that era of symbolism, mysticism, impressionism, *vers libre,* and decadence came much of his own philosophy and style. The spark of revolt and experiment in such names as Verlaine, Laforgue,

GERTRUDE STEIN, CARL VAN VECHTEN, AND ALICE B. TOKLAS, PHOTOGRAPHED BY VAN VECHTEN, NEW YORK, JANUARY 9, 1935

55

Rimbaud, Huysmans, George Moore, Mallarmé, Renoir, Degas, Manet, and Monet would be sufficient to demand his attention and win his loyalty. Indeed, the circus character of their defiance in life and art led him to characterize their "strange acrobatics" as "absinthe on the high wire."[1] But beneath the attraction of their novelty and color, Van Vechten recognized the spirit and the mission of the French impressionists, and in his own work he reflected these for an American public which did not yet understand the transition in the arts from nineteenth-century sentimental exposition to twentieth-century aesthetic evocation. England had long before caught the virus through the aesthetic hedonism of Pater, Swinburne, the Pre-Raphaelites, and Oscar Wilde, but in America, despite the work of Huneker, Saltus, and a handful of others, the change came late and virtually unannounced. There are no manifestos in American literature to match dadaist Tristan Tzara's ironic "We want works, straightforward, strong, accurate, and forever not understood," or Pater's counsel "to burn with a hard, gem-like flame," or Flaubert's slavery to the inevitable word, or Wilde's monumental disdain for traditional habit in Dorian Gray: "I cannot repeat an emotion. No one can, except sentimentalists."

The ferment was delayed in America until our whole social and intellectual being became vulnerable to revolt and experiment. The second and third decades of our century provided the atmosphere, and American artists, finally yielding to a kind of artificial insemination, brought the impressionist, the symbolist, the aesthete, and the stylist into our strain. The germ produced mutations as varied in appearance and color as Amy Lowell and the imagists, T. S. Eliot's *The Waste Land,* Gertrude Stein, Sherwood Anderson, Vachel Lindsay, Wallace Stevens, and William Faulkner.

Literary critics and historians, who could hardly ignore the inspiration of French free verse, have usually emphasized its influence while writing of our new poetry, sometimes obscuring its original values in the

---

1. It is interesting in this respect that Van Vechten's most fantastic and unconventional hero, Gunnar O'Grady in *Firecrackers,* is by profession an acrobat.

process. But the same critics and historians, partially blinded by the issues which inspired the novels of social consciousness and by the disturbing personalities of individual egos in fiction, have discussed the relation of our prose to this Continental revolution in the arts largely in terms of one literary creed: naturalism. Seldom do they give adequate recognition to the influence of the symbolist, the impressionist, the craftsman devoted to the perfection of each individual effect in his art, and the aesthetic connoisseur devoted to the ultimate expression of his refinements in taste. These artists, of course, emphasized disciplines leading to that enigmatic entity with the inadequate name—style.

As a result of the critics' narrowness, the present generation of novelists utilizes the achievements of its immediate precursors, often without knowing in what jeopardy this inheritance stood during the Twenties. Relatively few of the preceding generation of writers seem to have realized that the European revolt was their main source of inspiration and strength, that the fire in their own literature was not attributable simply to spontaneous combustion in America. For those who did recognize their legacy, much of this awareness came from the anecdotes, the cosmopolitan affinities, the critical appraisals, the familiar allusions, and the personal tastes of two Americans: James Huneker and Carl Van Vechten.

Huneker's contribution in this respect is undoubtedly the greater. It came earlier and is much the more substantial. Van Vechten's, however, has its own importance in point of time and content, coinciding with a national revolt from nineteenth-century tradition and decorum which met, and may have diminished, Huneker's enthusiasm. Van Vechten catered to an interest in the innovations of Continental culture growing out of our experience in World War I, and drew his audience partly from the inclination of a disillusioned society to seek release in worldliness and sophistication. Huneker was perhaps too close to the ideal, a Parisian— or better, a true Cosmopolitan; Van Vechten, who recorded his cultivated tastes and experiences with the exuberance of initiated youth and who found in New York lively competition for Old World manners and accomplishments, was always a cosmopolitan American.

2. THE STRANGE AND UNUSUAL have always attracted Carl Van Vechten. His patronage of the French symbolist-impressionist artists and the Parisian scene is only one aspect of a writing career devoted to the introduction of significant novelty and rare individuality in literature. Through his companionable essays, his novels, and his personal endorsements to literary friends and acquaintances, he sought a deserved audience for those artists whose eccentricity or departure from the traditional standards stood between them and the publisher or the reader, or both. There is in this part of Van Vechten's work both the honest satisfaction of championing a laudable cause and the perverse pleasure of turning up jolting contrasts to accepted literary fare. In each instance his reader senses the ascendancy of one purpose or the other, although both are always present. Few critics have devoted their essays so often and so pleasurably to searching out worthwhile oddities and diverting accomplishments in the work of little-known writers. Van Vechten had no fear of working the well dry. "I can always look back and discover a new face," he wrote. "At ninety I expect to sit before my fire, dallying amorously with some overlooked masterpiece."

Van Vechten's most persistent service in this vein grew out of his early experience in pre-World War I Paris. Since their first meeting he has been a champion of Gertrude Stein. Miss Stein has, in her appreciation of Van Vechten's help, given him credit for her first publication in America. Actually, he did arrange for the appearance of *Tender Buttons,* her second book to be published here, but *Three Lives* appeared before he knew her. Once he had discovered Gertrude Stein and her work, however, he became her consistent supporter. He was responsible for her entry into several American magazines. He took her *The Making of Americans* to Alfred A. Knopf, his own publisher, in an attempt to secure its publication, and, in the words of Miss Stein, "It was he who in one of his early books printed as a motto [for his essay on Mary Garden in *Interpreters and Interpretations*] the device on Gertrude Stein's notepaper, A rose is a rose is a rose is a rose." Through the years when her work provoked either derision or polite bewilderment, Van Vechten, experienced as a middleman between eccentric artist and reluctant public, kept it alive and in print. He squired her from Paris to Chicago for the performance of her opera *Four Saints in Three Acts,* with music by Virgil Thomson, and saw her faithfully through her 1935 lecture tour of America.

Since her death, he has assumed the task of editing the work of Gertrude Stein, and much of her uncollected material has already been published with his appreciative introductions. He has arranged for the publication of Miss Stein's very first book manuscript, *Things as They Are,* which had remained unpublished for nearly fifty years. Gertrude Stein died on July 27, 1946. Before this date, Van Vechten had edited, with an introduction and notes, the *Selected Writings of Gertrude Stein,* but the book did not reach the public until after her death. Publication of her *Last Operas and Plays* followed three years later, edited and with an introduction by Carl Van Vechten. As her literary executor, he has devoted much of his energy since her death to completing our record of Gertrude Stein both in print and on the stage. Reporting a production of her *Dr. Faustus Lights the Lights* by the Living Theatre in December, 1951 (for which he contributed program notes), Van Vechten wrote, "Dr. Faustus was much more interesting than I had hoped. The staging and the direction were excellent, and the music [by Richard Banks] good, and the audience behaved as if it were used to seeing Stein every night and liking it."

In 1921, when the revival of Herman Melville was under way, Van Vechten, although he paid his tributes unstintingly to *Moby Dick* and the better-known novels,[2] wrote with sympathy and special appreciation of the later work of that author. It is not surprising that *Pierre, The Confidence Man, Israel Potter,* and the *Piazza Tales* are still being "discovered"; indeed, the scholarly critics are only now giving these unique productions the careful inspection they deserve. "These books

2. In a review of Raymond Weaver's *Herman Melville: Mariner and Mystic,* for the *New York Evening Post* (Dec. 31, 1921), Van Vechten wrote, "it no longer can be said that no biography exists of the most brilliant figure in the history of our letters, the author of a book which far surpasses every other work created by an American from *The Scarlet Letter* to *The Golden Bowl.* For *Moby Dick* stands with the great classics of all times, with the tragedies of the Greeks, with Don Quixote, with Dante's *Inferno* and with Shakespeare's *Hamlet.*"

cannot be investigated by the aid of the critical jargon ordinarily applicable to works of art: they are the man himself," Van Vechten wrote in his essay on Melville. "Readers who are satisfied to stop with *Moby Dick* will not understand his later life, but those who go on . . . will get a clearer picture of his bitterness and unhappy striving."

American readers knew next to nothing of an English writer named Ronald Firbank until Carl Van Vechten, inevitably attracted to a prose which went off like erratic firecrackers in splashes of illumination, celebrated his unique fiction. Until *Prancing Nigger* was published here with the help of Van Vechten in 1924, Firbank was available in America only to the few who had access to his London editions. Earlier Van Vechten essays in praise of Firbank had appeared in 1922 and 1923, and were afterwards reprinted in *Excavations*.

Firbank's prose was the sort of impish art which fitted no known category and defied successful imitation. So unique and esoteric as to be almost incoherent, Firbank's style still revealed to a discerning reader a substance and core as wry and ironic as its bewildering flashes of imagination. What stood between writer and reader was this prodigious imagination which challenged the reader to provide his own light for the intervals of blackness between flashes. Firbank ignored them. The usual persistence of vision which could make smooth motion out of projected moving pictures failed the reader of Ronald Firbank. His sequences provided no consistent pattern, thriving instead on irregularity.

Van Vechten was delighted with such an art, impressed with the airy flippancy and the imaginative skill of this "glittering dragon-fly skimming over the sunlit literary garden, where almost all the other creatures crawl." He did what he could to share his pleasure with others. Over the objections of H. L. Mencken, he convinced Emily Clark, then editor of *The Reviewer,* that she should publish Firbank. He wrote encomiastic reviews which almost matched the jaunty temperament of Firbank's work. One described how on mail days traffic would be suspended around the Holliday Bookshop owing to crowds trying to get Firbank's books. According to Grant Richards, Firbank's publisher, that author took it literally in England, wrote Van Vechten, and received a reply "to the effect that if he would go to New York many thousands would flock to his lectures and many scores would meet him at the pier. And, Van Vechten added, if he would but publish his books in America he would sell thousands. . . ." In 1924, Brentano's edition of Firbank's *Prancing Nigger* carried a preface by Van Vechten, who had suggested the title. While the reception of Firbank's peculiar genius will never match Van Vechten's capricious predictions, his reputation continues to grow today. The publication of two Ronald Firbank volumes, *Five Novels* (1949) and *Three Novels* (1951), by New Directions has introduced his work to a second generation of readers.

In 1922, Carl Van Vechten could write with more truth than modesty, "With my own hands I have exhumed the skeleton of Edgar Saltus, arranging its fantastic contours in a corner of my museum, with the satisfactory result that the author of the Anatomy of Negation has become a favorite with 'collectors,' and is even read belatedly by a few adventurous spirits." The reference is to his 1918 essay on Saltus which appeared originally in *The Merry-Go-Round* and later joined the literary advocacies of *Excavations*. Van Vechten's figure of speech is accurate despite the fact that Saltus, who died in 1921, was still alive when the article was written. Saltus had played almost all his literary scenes off-stage. The brief vogue which his essays and novels enjoyed at the end of the century was due chiefly to their sensationalism and the contemporary legends of their author's own bohemian existence. Thereafter they lived only in the respect of a cultivated few who kept the faith in silence. James Huneker and Vance Thompson both considered doing a definitive article on Saltus, but the silence persisted until Van Vechten revealed the lush colors that lay under twenty years of dust. What he had discovered was not the great American master of prose, but a strikingly singular figure in our literature, virtually the only one whose work carried the genuine stamp of French impressionism and decadence in the contemporaneous American era.

Style is both the strength and the weakness of Saltus' work, for at its best it is sensitive, suggestive, amazingly careful expression, while in its self-conscious excess it caricatures itself. It often shrouds its subject in a suffusion of color and sensation, appearing to exist merely for the sake of its own effects and artifice. This preoccupation with style has led some critics to dispense with Saltus as a futile, isolated eccentric, or to excoriate him, as Oscar Cargill has done by labelling him "the unrivalled champion of bad taste, the promoter of frippery, the hen-feathered knight of vulgarity," who "carefully selected from the booty of the whole world only the inutile and fantastic to dump on our shores." Such a pronouncement is not without its application to the more florid and involuted aspects of Saltus' writing, but it denies the place of anything "inutile and fantastic" in our literature. It ignores the impelling presence of the art-for-art's-sake principle in one of its earliest American exponents, and it glosses with abuse the introduction of Continental *fin-de-siècle* art to a people who, like the natives of Maple Valley, Iowa, in *The Tattooed Countess,* understood the French term as roughly equivalent to "the latest thing."

Van Vechten's acceptance of Edgar Saltus is avowedly one of personal taste, a taste acquired from sources similar to those of Saltus. It is this affinity, however, which allows Van Vechten to vouch for the authenticity of the earlier stylist, to review him in his context of time and literary milieu. While his praise of Saltus is probably inordinate by most critical standards, it is by no means blind. Without minimizing the personal appeal Saltus' prose held for him, he could admit, "At his worst— and his worst could be monstrous!—garbed fantastically in purple patches and gaudy rags, he wallows in muddy puddles of Burgundy and gold dust."

It was the same champion of the misunderstood and undersung who called for contemporary recognition of Henry Blake Fuller, whom he found "perhaps not the greatest of living American novelists, but certainly one of the most original and distinguished." Fuller was not without other champions: Robert Morss Lovett, H. L. Mencken, Percival Pollard, and Huneker were some who had shown their appreciation. But Van Vechten's appraisal was a broadside estimate calculated to stimulate a wider interest in an artist who had told him further novels were unlikely: they took too much effort and gave too little return. Fuller is seen

Carl Van Vechten

as a disappointed cosmopolitan, "mired in Chicago," preferring Italy, and writing sensitively and effectively of both. Quoting examples, Van Vechten pointed to Fuller's civilized sense of humor, delicate, polished, and sufficiently ironic to make a maximum of effect with a minimum of effort.

> Fuller's touch is like the lifting of an eyebrow, the quick flick of an ash from a cigarette, a gentle tapping of a boot on a not too resounding pavement. A sensitive reader will perhaps react to these peaceful signals more graciously than to the more emphatic outcries of a Theodore Dreiser. Fuller's humor never exacts a great guffaw, or his pathos a flood of tears. He is quietly amusing and gently melancholy.

Twenty years later, Alfred Kazin, placing Fuller among the early "metropolitan realists" in his survey of modern American prose, *On Native Grounds,* dwelt on the same qualities that set Fuller apart from the others in his group. To Kazin, "the gentle little man who abominated Chicago" had an "exquisite soul," the mark of "a graceful and impressionistic artist" who "could write skillfully, with a lambent touch that mocked his own bitterness; his flip style and loosely sardonic craftsmanship even anticipated the sophisticated novel of the nineteen-twenties."

Not all Van Vechten's literary excavations have a sense of mission. More consistent with his own random style and whimsicality are the essays which turn up romantic figures with the appeal of spirit, dash, and nonchalant accomplishment. In approaching the novels of Ouida, for instance, he writes that he was "weary of modern fiction, tainted with Freud and Fabre, weary of James Joyce and Dorothy Richardson and D. H. Lawrence, weary of Romain Rolland and his quest for a perfect world." The list might be extended at some length.

The mood must be a familiar one to many a bookman. Marcel Proust and Thomas Wolfe, along with Rolland, each are capable of bringing it on alone if taken at a gulp. Two courses are open to the victim, an escape from books or an escape in books. Van Vechten took the latter. "It has long been a contention of mine," he wrote with a bland lack of qualification, "that middle-class life is as dull in art as it is in reality. Ouida, seemingly, agreed with me." Philip Thicknesse, Matthew Phipps Shiel, and the other authors whose writings he sought when in such a mood also agreed with him.

The well-adjusted superman, the superior-being in mufti, has always been a favorite of Van Vechten's. The penchant for such fictional figures, cast in real or fanciful molds, may be traced back to his boyhood adoration of Horatio Alger, Jr., and Ingersoll Lockwood. Certainly there is a pattern to be discerned in his enthusiasm for Ouida's daring guardsmen; the eighteenth-century Philip Thicknesse, "an irascible and cultivated English gentleman-adventurer with a kind of genius for expressing himself"; the world-conquering Richard Hogarth of M. P. Shiel's *Lord of the Sea;* the dauntless, intrepid Gerald of Elinor Wylie's *Jennifer Lorn;* and his own Gunnar O'Grady of *Firecrackers.* In a sense Van Vechten's Peter Whiffle and Campaspe Lorillard can be added to the list.

Van Vechten wrote affectionately of all these entertaining figures. In the case of Miss Wylie's *Jennifer Lorn,* he encountered the naïve Jennifer and her peerless Gerald set in an urbane, delightfully ironic and subtle prose that enhanced their appeal immeasurably. The combination overwhelmed him. He announced its perfection to every available ear. Besides talking and writing of his enthusiasm, he led a torchlight procession through the streets of New York to honor the appearance of the novel. When *The Collected Prose of Elinor Wylie* was released in 1946, his introduction to *Jennifer Lorn* held undiminished appreciation. Twenty-three years earlier, Elinor Wylie had written in his copy: "For Carl Van Vechten, without whom this book would never have been read."

Many others might write similar inscriptions on their work, for Van Vechten has been New York's town crier on numerous occasions. He read the poems of Langston Hughes, whom he had met at an N.A.A.C.P. benefit party in Harlem, and submitted them to A. A. Knopf. They were published as *The Weary Blues.* Hughes reciprocated by supplying the snatches of blues for *Nigger Heaven,* and by appreciative mention of Van Vechten's many services in his autobiography, *The*

Big Sea. Alfred Knopf often relied on Van Vechten's judgment entirely in decisions about manuscripts. Among the others recommended to him by Van Vechten, Knopf lists authors James Weldon Johnson and Rudolph Fisher; artist-writer Miguel Covarrubias; poet Wallace Stevens; and novelists Neith Boyce, Isa Glenn, M. P. Shiel, Chester Himes, H. B. Fuller, and Arthur Machen.

As a comfortable supplement to the essays which celebrate other writers who had pleased him, a number of Van Vechten's literary essays center about no one topic but wander amiably among a series of points in focus. One of these essays, "The Holy Jumpers" from *In the Garret*, is a good example of this Van Vechten method. Opening with the author's consideration of personal pleasures and thrills, it moves to a comfortable, vivid description-appreciation of Nassau and vicinity in the Bahamas, and finally leaps into a frenzied account in staccato, impressionistic prose of the evangelistic fervor of those islands' Negro "Holy Jumpers." His talent for light, entertaining, and informative essays is demonstrated by "On Visiting Fashionable Places Out of Season" and "A Note on Dedications," the opening and closing offerings in *Excavations*. Both of these display the bookman who composed them, but both are characteristically free of the bookish restraint and stiltedness that so often accompany such essays.

All of Van Vechten's essays offer the flavor of a distinct literary personality. His discourse allows no separation from its author, for it follows the whim of writer rather than reader with only such unbending as comes naturally from the amiability of the former. It maintains a quality of detached individuality which forever leads its reader toward a complete rapport but persistently eludes him in some sophisticated or allusive maneuver. The writer refuses to stand still and remains beyond the reach of traditional demands on literary criticism. Much of the strength and appeal of his writing dwells in this quality, for, as the *New York Times* review of *Excavations* observed, "To dismiss him airily with some remark about pastiche means nothing, for Mr. Van Vechten has already dismissed you with an airiness that it will take you much practice to achieve."

3. IN HIS FAREWELL to music criticism, Van Vechten referred to himself as "a writer who apparently at heart was always creative rather than critical." The assertion is borne out by his earlier writing and indicates the comparative ease with which he underwent the metamorphosis from critic to novelist. The groundwork for his fiction is evident in his essays. A number of the essays written in the year preceding *Peter Whiffle*, his first novel, were frankly experiments in narrative. The creation of vivid description and atmosphere had become more and more the mark of his sketches. The writing career of James Huneker followed a similar pattern, except that the short fictions published with his critical essays were more clearly set apart, and his first novel, *Painted Veils* (written when Huneker was in his sixties) was also his last.

Van Vechten's transition to fiction was also cushioned by the presentation of two books about cats, *The Tiger in the House* in 1920, and *Lords of the Housetops,* a collection of stories which he edited in 1921. The first of these is an encyclopedia of cat lore that stands by itself as the most complete and indisputably literary study of its subject in our literature. The book has been reissued four times, its quaintness and readability making it the standard favorite of cat lovers for two generations, as comprehensive and entertaining for readers of its 1950 edition as it was for its English and American audience in 1920. In its thorough consideration of feline manner and psychology, the book was especially germane to the enigmatic, graceful philosophy of individual detachment which was to command the sophisticated characters and situations of his novels, and which was to be pointedly symbolized in *Peter Whiffle* by the austere self-containment and complete subjective unity of the cat. His preface for Svend Fleuron's *Kittens* in 1922 and the simple, sensitive tribute to his own Persian cat, *Feathers,* published as a Random House Quarto in 1930, were to round out the literary contributions of puss's most articulate student and champion in America.

His affection for cats remained boundless, but Van Vechten ended ties with his own pets some time ago. Visitors noting the absence of cats in the Van Vechten apartment are reassured. "Attachments to my cats," he has said, "ran too deep. I missed them too much when they were gone."

4. BEFORE HE RETIRED HIS PEN in favor of his camera, Van Vechten published seven novels in almost annual succession. Like the criticism that went before them, they shocked some, titillated others, and charmed many. The latter group was all the audience he was concerned with. Emily Clark's portrait in *Innocence Abroad* states that all he desired when a new book of his was given life was "that a special group of people who may exist in any part of the world shall say with a true pleasure and anticipation: 'Here is another Van Vechten.' "

Peter Whiffle: His Life and Works, conceived—according to its author—in the winter of 1920 and brought to the public in 1922, catapulted him into the ranks of popular novelists. Its novelty as a half-valid biography was engaging, its scenes were romantic and worldly, its style was the pleasing union of ease, wit, and knowledge, and it carried its burden with a lightness difficult to attain in any artistic performance. "The *Bookman's* Guide to Fiction" for June, 1922, a feature of the magazine which listed the titles of current novels with a sentence or two of description, recommended *Peter Whiffle* with the extravagant comment, "Enthralling truth beneath the cosmetics of fiction. Gloriously real and written well." Another entry on the same list reveals, by contrast, some measure of the appeal and impact of Van Vechten's novel at that time. John Dos Passos' *Three Soldiers* was described bluntly as "Three malcontents in a vivid war setting."

The phrase "gloriously real," could have reference to the presence in the novel of persons who, as the book's dust jacket puts it, "appear under their own names" while "others wear thin epithetical masks." This same jacket begins its blurb with the challenging query, "Who was Peter Whiffle?" The question may have seemed a vital one then, but it has become largely rhetorical now, without minimizing the quality or interest of the novel at all. Possibly it enhances it for readers who find in the duet of Carl, the biographer, and Peter, the subject, a kind of Jekyll and Hyde artistic schizophrenia, the former recording sympathetically but honestly the excess and folly of the latter. For Peter is the author who never wrote a book, the heady pursuer of the strange, the occult, the remote, the exquisite, the aesthetic moment, and the perpetual escape from encroaching boredom: in short, a calculated distortion of the incubi which beckoned to Carl Van Vechten.[3]

Such a reading is, indeed, supported almost literally in some respects. On pages 147 and 148, Carl discovers Peter attired in "a white silk shirt, a tie of Chinese blue brocade, clasped with a black opal" and wearing as a ring "an amethyst intaglio, with Leda and the Swan as its subject." Mabel Dodge Luhan recalls in her *Intimate Memories* that "Carl's soft silk shirt had turned-back cuffs ... buttoned with bold links that had some dull, half-precious stones embedded sleepily there in the shining metal ... He wore a merry intaglio depicting Leda and the swan, set in a gold ring ... and his neckties came from Fifth Avenue shops." Later in the novel, Carl explains that Peter gave the ring to him, but it seems certain that Mabel Dodge was describing Van Vechten at an earlier date than 1917 or 1918. The death of Peter, announced in the opening sentence as occurring almost unnoticed in the winter of 1919-1920, would represent Carl's decision to write Peter's book, ending his subject's fruitless existence in the process. Van Vechten's preface, in which he explains his relation to Peter and his position as literary executor, assumes the flavor of clever ambiguity, and the final dialogue in Peter's (therefore Carl's) New York apartment, climaxed by his quiet cessation, takes on added strength and appropriateness. Appealing as such an interpretation might be, however, account must be taken of two references to Peter in previous works; in the essay on Philip Thicknesse (November, 1918): "Perhaps when I am through with my books Peter Whiffle, who now ardently desires my set of Lafcadio Hearn, may be browsing in other fields," and in "La Tigresse" of *In the Garret* (February, 1919): "I cannot get along without knowing Peter Whiffle."

Regardless of Peter's role as shadow or substance, the tale of his feverish, scattershot existence is unusual in American literature. That it

3. Neith Boyce, an intimate friend and companion both in this country and abroad, wrote Van Vechten in a letter of 1922 about both the autobiographical representation and the elusive personality of the novel: "... it is more *you* than anything else of yours I've read, and therefore has charm and something else which I've never decided just what it is."

would not be unique in French or English literature is an indication of a good deal of its significance in ours. J. K. Huysmans' *A Rebours* and Oscar Wilde's *The Picture of Dorian Gray* are clearly stepfather and half brother, respectively, to *Peter Whiffle*.

The relation to *A Rebours* is the more secure of the two, for unlike Wilde, Huysmans and Van Vechten both observe their decadent hero with sympathetic detachment. They identify themselves only with the attractions of their heroes, not with the heroes themselves, in this manner emerging allied to but separate from them. With this superior sophistication they can satirize without choosing sides; they can indulge themselves without abandoning themselves to that indulgence. Huysmans accomplishes this more subtly, Van Vechten more cleverly, but each avoids the passionate self-involvement that gives *The Picture of Dorian Gray* its brilliant but hideous genius. The Frenchman and the American wrote parody, the Englishman tragedy.

A catalogue of the similarities between Huysmans' hero and Peter Whiffle illustrates the original treatment accorded the latter. Both seek, through strange byways, ultimate sensation and revelation, but Des Esseintes desires the experience for its own sake, while Peter wishes to utilize it in art. Des Esseintes, desiring to visit England, does so by intellectually detaching himself from his French surroundings and *imagining* England; the more impetuous Peter's false starts to Bermuda, Europe, and other beckoning lands melt in the conclusion that "I am not compelled to go anywhere; I can stay on right here." The accounts of mystic, diabolic, horrific rites read by Peter Whiffle out of "Dr. Braitaille's Le Diable au XIXe Siècle" outdo the efforts of Huysmans in imaginative grossness, but in all details Van Vechten maintains the basic humor of their excess— closer to James Branch Cabell in this respect than to Huysmans. When Peter concludes the selection "with an expression of ironic exultation," his biographer is asked what he thinks of it. "Very pretty," he ventures. When each of the drugs which Peter takes for the mystic powers of divination and vision has a violently unhealthy, opposite effect, completely denying the powers of mind in the ensuing physical illness, he is bewildered and humanly discouraged; disease is foreign to him. Des Esseintes seems most in character when prostrated by exhaustion and self-inflicted physical debility. Most indicative of all is the climax of Peter's esoteric experiments—the near farce of a very real explosion which lands both experimenter and observer in a very real hospital.

Des Esseintes, troubled by the religious doubts of the Old World grown too civilized, too refined, stalks Death; Peter Whiffle, troubled only with youthful confusion, indecision, and doubts of his own capability, seeks—and finds—his answers in Life. Each, in a dream brought on by physical proximity to death, encounters the personification of that inevitability. Des Esseintes' is a horrifying nightmare describing in pulse-raising prose his maddening pursuit by the image of the Pox: "The ambiguous, sexless creature was green, and from under purple lids shown a pair of pale blue eyes, cold and terrible; two arms of an inordinate leanness, like a skeleton's bare to the elbows, shaking with fever, projected from ragged sleeves, and the fleshless thighs shuddered in churn-boots, a world too wide." To Peter Whiffle, Death—"A woman in a rusty black robe" which "confused itself in my mind with Kathleen-ni-Houlihan and (will you believe it?) Sara Allgood!"—waits impatiently while an Angel and the Devil plead, like California and Florida real estate agents, the advantages of their respective realms. Peter dispels all three with the realization of the laissez-faire personal philosophy which punctuates the novel like a refrain, *"I was not compelled to go anywhere."*

Peter Whiffle is able to lift himself from the oppression of his obsessions. Hope for Des Esseintes is a mocking ghost, although his creator found it again in Roman Catholicism. Part of Peter's last discussion with Carl deserves quotation for the light it throws on both Peter Whiffle and his creator:

> I am not complaining or asking for sympathy. I am explaining how I felt, not how I feel. I never spoke of it, of course, while I felt that way. I am only talking about it now because I have gone beyond, because, in a sense, at least, I understand. I am happier now, happier, perhaps, than I have ever been before, for in the

Carl Van Vechten

past four years I have left behind my restlessness and achieved something like peace. I no longer feel that I have failed. Of course, I have failed, but that was because I was attempting to do something that I had no right to attempt. . . . It is necessary to do only what one must, what one is forced by nature to do.

The search for a working philosophy and a sense of identity in *Peter Whiffle* has a timeless appeal, and qualifies among the most lasting elements in Van Vechten's fiction. A letter from Thomas Beer to Van Vechten in 1922 commented succinctly on this core of the novel: "Dear Van Vechten—My aunt has read Peter Whiffle and says that it contains a good moral lesson. Yours, Thomas Beer."

But the novel had more to offer its reader in 1922—and subsequent readers interested in that time. It presented Paris through the enchanted eyes of one of the Americans who knew it best. It guided the reader on a sophisticate's tour of the city which had grown fabulous with the tales of returning doughboys. It catalogued the dream so many Americans cherished of being dropped in the midst of that uninhibited, cosmopolitan scene. "An American youth's first view of Paris," Robert Morss Lovett has written, "is an unforgettable experience, a favorite theme of Henry James, but nowhere touched on so happily as by Carl Van Vechten in *Peter Whiffle*."

The novel also offered ringside seats at the show, part comic, part serious, put on by the intellectuals who populated the revolving scenes of New York and the Continent. The salon gatherings of Mabel Dodge were reported, with lively discussions of art, politics, social problems, life, death, and matters in between, providing entertaining respite neatly tied to the narrative of Peter's "life and work." A serious appraisal of the mystic novels written by the little known Arthur Machen stirred up a recognition of that strange stylist that has been renewed by periodic revivals ever since. "The most wonderful man writing English today and nobody knows him!" exclaimed Peter, and Carl gave five pages to his further remarks on the peculiar art of Machen.

It offered all this in prose that, with all its mania for cataloguing remote nomenclatures and dredging various seas of pseudo-scientific terminology, read with the lightness and grace of a comic ballet. Quotation marks and interrupting punctuation were dispensed with, as if the author had carried over into his prose the effects of Erik Satie's lack of bar lines in the music Van Vechten prized so much. As the author himself wrote of Satie's style: "There are no separations. Nothing is dichotomized . . . . The music runs along."

Peter Whiffle was a remarkable first novel, even considering the apprenticeship its author served in his essays. It is Van Vechten's signal, but by no means his single, achievement in fiction.

5. WITH THE SUCCESS of Peter Whiffle, Van Vechten was acclaimed a novelist and "sat down to write, with the greatest of ease, The Blind Bow-Boy." During its preparation, the author kept his friend Emily Clark informed of its progress. In July, 1922, he told her that he was "writing a new novel which is amusing me so much that I absolve it from the need of amusing future readers." Again: "My formula at present consists in treating extremely serious themes as frivolously as possible. Doubtless when I am eighty I shall be able to write like Sherwood Anderson, if you want me to." Later: ". . . it is a strange opus, wreathed in masks and smiles and false cues and bandages and yet open-faced as an Ingersoll." Finally, in 1923: "It is a nice book. If Ben Hecht had written it, it could be called *devastating,* but I shall make it charming."

Such a book had the seeds of controversy. The reviews brought them to flower. Some placed Van Vechten ceremoniously in company with the sophisticated progeny of Thomas Love Peacock, and wielded names noticeably foreign to American literature to make their point. "Beside Floyd Dell and Willa Cather," wrote Edmund Wilson, "he is Ariel, Till Eulenspiegel." Ernest Boyd applauded its civilized humor and detachment: "After so many volumes of morbid introspection or of adolescent revolt, it is a relief to be assured that there are people in this country so happily unaware of the alleged disadvantages of being an American, who are not overpowered by a sense of their own identity."

Others lamented the new perversity and nastiness, however light and readable, in the author of the brilliant *Peter Whiffle*. An amusing and enlightening squabble took place in the pages of the *Bookman*. A review of the disappointed variety, signed "J. F." (John Farrar), concluded: "It is neither very good as a shocker nor very penetrating as a satire . . . and if you are a really nice person, you will not understand a great deal of it, thank heaven! What a pity for a man who can write so well to write such a sublimated edition of a Broadway scandal sheet." In a subsequent issue, a "Miss E. D." took him to task in a letter which asserted, "The difference [between Van Vechten, D. H. Lawrence, Sherwood Anderson, and the other 'nasties'] is that the 'Bow-Boy' is not pretending to be serious, and the others are. Van Vechten is at his best in a light, satirical vein and being a modern young man he cannot possibly write a novel that does not deal largely with sex." Farrar generously overlooked the non sequitur and forgot *Peter Whiffle*, replying that she "couldn't possibly have understood Mr. Van Vechten's book," and recommending "that she have it carefully interpreted to her by, say, an eminent psychologist."

The story itself is a revised version of The Rake's Progress. Harold Prewett, a youth fresh from college, unassailed in his innocence by worldly experience or knowledge, is deposited by his father in the midst of New York's most sophisticated, uninhibited society, revolving around its curiously detached queen, Campaspe Lorillard, ostensibly to replace with more serviceable experience in the ways of life the cloistered education ordered by his mother. When it is revealed to Harold that the experiment was meant to turn him forever against the temptations of such high life, he resents his father's duplicity, embraces the experiences which had formerly been so repulsive to him, and announces his preference for the company of the uninhibited sect which had accepted him honestly. The worldly education of the innocent is completed in the last line of the novel when Campaspe, bound for Europe, discovers on her ship the erstwhile lamb, Harold Prewett, outward bound with the infamous Duke of Middlebottom, the most perverse member of her realm, as his traveling companion.

Readers beguiled by the book's title, by the name of its heroine, and by the presence of her pitiful husband, nicknamed "Cupid," may have recalled that Campaspe was the beautiful concubine of Alexander the Great, given by the king to the artist Apelles, who had fallen in love with her as he painted her picture. They may have inferred that Van Vechten's Campaspe was given only to her creator since she will have none of any of the willing male characters in the book, least of all her adoring husband. If they referred to the airy song that closes the last scene of Act III in John Lyly's Elizabethan dramatization, *Alexander and Campaspe,* they learned that the surpassing lady completely bested Cupid in a game of chance, divesting him in the final wager of both his eyes, vouchsafing him his legendary blindness and providing an arresting title for Carl Van Vechten. The song is rendered by Apelles, who has not yet been awarded Campaspe:

> Cupid and my Campaspe playd
> At Cardes for kisses, Cupid payd;
> He stakes his quiuer, Bow & Arrows,
> His Mothers doues, & teeme of sparows;
> Looses them too; then, downe he throwes
> The corrall of his lippe, the rose
> Growing on's cheek (but none knows how),
> With these, the cristall of his Brow,
> And then the dimple of his chinne:
> All these did my Campaspe winne.
> At last, hee set her both his eyes;
> Shee won, and Cupid blind did rise.
>> O Loue! has shee done this to Thee?
>> What shall (Alas!) become of mee?

This legend had attracted Van Vechten as early as 1904, when he wrote music for "Cupid and Campaspe," included in his collection of songs, *Five Old English Ditties*.

In the novel, the author symbolizes this theme rather too patently through occasional references to the statue of the blindfolded Eros which stands in the center of Campaspe's patio. In the narrative, if the term can be used for such a whirling merry-go-round of action, the capricious bow-boy is truly blind. Harold Prewett shifts from the proper Alice Blake to the improper Zimbule O'Grady in a week, with a respectful pass at the incomparable Campaspe sandwiched in between. Cupid Lorillard, frustrated by his wife's constant disdain and rejection, purchases a season ticket to Zimbule's bedroom, and the others in Campaspe's society exhibit no consistency—do not want any—in their amours.

The shocking aspects of *The Blind Bow-Boy* are not especially tasteful. They are delivered however, with humor and ironic purpose, and to the extent that these elements are paramount (they are not as consistently so as one might wish) their excess is acceptable. Campaspe does not *know* the vices, one of her friends remarks, she *invents* them. In a similar fashion, Van Vechten grants his own license in the manner he assumes: "A book, Campaspe considered, should have the swiftness of melodrama, the lightness of farce, to be a real contribution to thought . . . . How could anything serious be hidden more successfully than in a book which pretended to be light and gay?" At times, the gaiety of the proceedings does not appear functionally perverse, even though part of the guiding philosophy in the book is the cathartic amusement offered by the observation of perversity in others.

The underlying purpose of the book is reflected in its society of sophisticates who covet the outlandish in the knowledge that life and truth themselves are outlandish. They prefer to meet absurdity head on rather than have it eat away their lives by slow corrosion. The release implicit in such a creed is, to a certain extent, the explanation of the gaps between Van Vechten's first and second novels. Peter Whiffle's "Do what you have to do" had the ring of inevitability, but *The Blind Bow-Boy* altered it subtly to "Do what you will."

6. *THE SUBTITLE* for *The Blind Bow-Boy* was a phrase cleverly calculated to announce the serio-comic nature of the novel. Van Vechten called it "A Cartoon for a Stained-Glass Window." The phrase which accompanied his next novel, *The Tattooed Countess* (1924), was "A Romantic Novel with a Happy Ending." This subtitle, like everything else about its book, carried a broad irony which would have become gross in the hands of a writer less accomplished in the light touch.

The book joined many others of the Twenties in its portraiture of Small-Town America, but its approach was Van Vechten's own. Sinclair Lewis used a kind of satirical redundancy, cataloguing so many examples of unwitting buffoonery and shallowness in the small-town mind that it barely fell short of affectionate caricature. Floyd Dell chronicled, with a depressing atmosphere of vague frustration, the struggle of a sensitive young soul in the crass environment of urban provincialism. Sherwood Anderson moved inside the people themselves to reveal the tragedy, the intensity, and the emotional animation of the town. Van Vechten's novel combines all three of these methods and adds to the mixture the catalyst of pervading irony. Arthur Davidson Ficke, expressing his pleasure with *The Tattooed Countess* in a letter to its author, wrote: ". . . it is delightful to see Main Street described in terms of amusement instead of the usual terms of fury."

The tattooed countess is Ella Nattatorrini, widow of an Italian count, intimate of cosmopolitan scenes and societies, irrepressible lover of beautiful young men and of love itself. The novel opens on June 17, 1897 (the day on which Van Vechten was 17), with the return of this sophisticated but entirely human lady to the town of Maple Valley, Iowa, where, fifty years before, she had been born Ella Poore. It is her hope that her childhood scenes will help dispel the monumental grief resulting from her dismissal by the last of a series of Continental young men to whom she had devoted herself and her late husband's fortune.

The irony implicit in this situation is borne through the novel with a skillful use of modulation and a disciplined sense of form. Having given his reader the Countess in the opening scene, Van Vechten presents the town in the second chapter by recording the regular morning activity and conversation of two insignificant housewives, Mrs. Bierbauer and Mrs. Fox, whose barren lives, like their front porches, are separated only by a wooden fence. Introduced as local members of the Parcæ who "preside over human destinies in every town in the middle west," they reveal themselves much more adequately through their perfect dialogue and the fact that Mrs. Bierbauer's somnolent tomcat is named Trilby. The natural limits of the narrative having been reached with the climactic departure of the Countess, an epilogue returns the reader to the Parcæ and their perpetual rocking chair pronouncements.

The hasty exit of the Countess involves a figure who remained a peripheral character through the rest of Van Vechten's novels. Gareth Johns, who was to be an eminent novelist to the characters of later books, is the sensitive youth bound in by the provincialism and hypocrisy of the town. He is the only resident who prefers to conform to the Countess Nattatorrini rather than the other way around, and she is the only person in his life who can lead him, both figuratively and literally, beyond Maple Valley. This plus his youth and gender are sufficient to fulfill the purpose of the Countess in coming back to Maple Valley, but, ironically, her purpose is eventually to be accomplished only by leaving.

There is more than a little in Gareth Johns to suggest the young Van Vechten of Cedar Rapids. Gareth is, "paradoxically, of both a sentimental and cynical turn of mind." His activities and interests are consistently those that Van Vechten has recorded about himself elsewhere. He collects, for instance, mementos of theatrical celebrities and reads omnivorously in the same books that are recorded as Van Vechten's early literary fare. When he takes Lennie Colman, his aging high school teacher (whose painful infatuation for Gareth is the novel's moving personal tragedy) on a hunt for birds' eggs, she doesn't think he should take all the eggs (a "clutch") from any one nest. An autobiographical essay of 1921 recalls, "When I sought birds' eggs, my mother, picturing the despair of the mother bird, begged me to leave at least one egg in each nest I despoiled." The setting of time and place add weight to such evidence; but there is invention enough in the story to make autobiographical matter a valuable means of achieving verisimilitude and total effect.[4] Gareth Jones does escape into the world he seeks, as did Van Vechten, but the story of his escape is the work of art as well as of memory. The tragedy of Lennie Colman's life is a memorable instance of this invention. She is the sensitive soul who does *not* escape, the person qualified for life who lacks the strength and independence to *do what she wishes* to make of herself what she *is*.

The mixture of sentiment and cynicism in Gareth Johns is present in equal parts in the book. Like Sinclair Lewis, Van Vechten reveals an affection for the very scenes and people he satirizes. In 1918, he had written, "The Iowa scene has been infrequently described in literature and no writer, I think, has yet done justice to it." By 1924, a number of writers had discovered that scene. A year earlier, Roger L. Sergel set his study in psychological realism, *Arlie Gelston,* in an Iowa country town, utilizing the Iowa landscape and the village of Coon Falls. Ruth Suckow, whose work definitely abrogated Van Vechten's statement, had begun her stories of Iowa life as early as 1921, contributing to *The Midland* and *The Smart Set.* Van Vechten's contribution in 1924 gave his native state full status on the literary map of America.

This element of sentimental affection for the locale is, however, more than offset by the indictment of its society. The title of the book itself symbolizes the ironic contrasts which bare the soggy soul of the town. The Countess, who wears her heart on her sleeve, is appropriately tattooed on the arm with a token of dedication to her last young man. Her open honesty is matched by the secrecy and duplicity of the town. Comparing herself with the Maple Valley hypocrites, she observes that "I am tattooed on my arm while they are tattooed on their hearts." Van Vechten speaks of Maple Valley as a "provincial community where so many people were old because the young went away as soon as possible

---

4. Significantly, the relation is in the third person. First person point of view (something Van Vechten never attempted after its successful use in *Peter Whiffle*) would have made the exceptional form of *The Tattooed Countess* impossible. Omniscience was necessary, for example, to bring the Countess and the Parcæ before the reader with the special impact and balance of the two opening chapters.

to carry out their lives elsewhere." He has the Countess exclaim prophetically (for 1897): "The narrow prejudices of this town, based on a complete ignorance of life, are stifling .... I wonder ... if all America is like this? You'd better look out! You don't know what you're doing to the next generation. They won't stand it, no one with any brains would stand it! They'll revolt! They'll break loose!" This was the generation whose local future had been gloriously envisioned by Judge Porter, who turned the occasion of a welcoming address to the Countess into a splendidly ridiculous eulogy of the Maple Valley High School.

The ingredients of this novel are mixed with a fine sense of proportion and taste. Irony and humor are so nicely matched to a style of simplicity and wit that the story seldom seems to be carrying the burden of its own weight. Van Vechten's predilection for strange, unfamiliar words sprinkles the surface of his sentences, but this calculated eccentricity lends to his style a quality more piquant than precious.[5] In a letter to a Boston lady wishing advice for her son who desired to become a writer, W. Somerset Maugham wrote, on October 10, 1924:

> A novel should have an inner harmony and there is no reason why the reader should be deprived of the delight which he may obtain from a beautiful proportion. In this connection I strongly recommend your son to read Carl Van Vechten's "The Tattooed Countess." He will find in it a model of form which alone makes the book a pleasure to read; and he will find also ingenious characterization and an enchanting humor. He cannot read it attentively without obtaining from it valuable instruction, profit and edification. It is a perfect example of perhaps the most difficult book to write: the light novel.

5. Joseph Warren Beach in *The Outlook for American Prose* (1927) prints isolated excerpts from *The Tattooed Countess*, discredits the sophisticated style, and censures the use of individual words. Stanley Edgar Hyman in *The Armed Vision* (1948), while discussing the "teacher's close reading," cites "Joseph Warren Beach, in *The Outlook for American Prose* particularly, reading contemporary literature with the grammarian's little eye, and rewriting, in a 'corrected' form, passages from authors ... as though they were freshman themes."

With *The Tattooed Countess,* Van Vechten fashioned the links which were to connect all seven of his novels through the appearance in each book of one or more characters familiar in the plots of the others. The device was not new. Balzac and Edgar Saltus each had characters appearing in a number of novels. James Branch Cabell also presented a series, jumping generations and characters to round out a full picture. The interlocking nature of Van Vechten's series, however, seems to have no heavy pattern, no conscious over-all scheme. As a result, the reader of all seven novels gains the effect of a camera revolving over a panorama, but stopping here and there for a long, detailed closeup of a highlighted scene. As in the fluid comedy of television, the performers can wander blithely from one scene to its adjoining set; but unlike performers in that self-conscious medium, Van Vechten's characters appear at random, unannounced, at ease, and unaware of their own ubiquity. They are as content with a walk-on as they are with a leading role.

The first four novels comprise a set in confused order, with connections made backwards and forwards. Working in both directions from *The Tattooed Countess* (written third, but first in point of narrative chronology), Van Vechten reached *Peter Whiffle* through the presence of the young Clara Barnes, adolescent diva of Maple Valley, who was to continue her pursuit of the singer's art and fame in the cosmopolitan society of Carl and Peter, and through the Parisian life anticipated by Gareth Johns in his escape with the Countess. *Firecrackers,* the fourth novel, returned to the society of *The Blind Bow-Boy,* tracing further the careers of Campaspe, Paul Moody, and others of their sophisticated set. It reached back to *The Tattooed Countess* through the entrances of Gareth Johns (now a successful author of international notoriety and acclaim) and the final exit of the Countess Nattatorrini, whose extraordinary death scene is witnessed by her friend Campaspe Lorillard. Edith Dale, patroness of personalities and ideas in *Peter Whiffle,* is re-introduced in correspondence as Campaspe reads through her morning mail, and takes her curtain call offstage in the New Mexican scenes of the 1928 opus, *Spider Boy.* Mahalah Wiggins, whom Peter Whiffle almost married, is another character from that novel revived briefly when she turns up at a party in *Firecrackers*. (Mahalah is identified as an actress. Campaspe asks, "Where does she act?" "In an old-fashioned piece of furniture with four posts," is the reply.) Campaspe and Gareth Johns both enter the settings of *Nigger Heaven* as sympathetic whites briefly seen at Harlem occasions, and Johns carries the associations of former books and characters into the final novel, *Parties,* wherein he associates with Hamish Wilding at one of the interminable cocktail parties, and accompanies that young man afterwards to a Harlem apartment.

7. *IN HER ENTHUSIASM* for *The Tattooed Countess*, Gertrude Atherton, according to Scott Cunningham's *Chicago Evening Post* review of *Firecrackers,* Van Vechten's fourth novel, "swore a solemn oath that the author of 'The Tattooed Countess' would not be long for this world if his next book dealt not with the Parisian activities of that fin de siecle time and couple." In the opening paragraph of *Firecrackers,* Van Vechten cleverly parried the threat by picturing the impatience of Paul Moody with a novel identifiable to the reader without benefit of titles as a sequel to or continuation of *The Tattooed Countess* (Campaspe later reveals the author: Gareth Johns). It "dealt with a young American boy kept by a rich woman in her middle years" and "was, Paul felt rather than thought, too much like life to be altogether agreeable." He decided he could not suffer it further perusal. In this fashion, Van Vechten explains his return to the speed, gaiety, and fantasy of *The Blind Bow-Boy* crowd. Further on, he has Gareth Johns defend it in a discussion which has its bearing on all his fiction:

> It doesn't seem to occur to the crowd that it is possible for an
> author to believe that life is largely without excuse, that if there
> is a God he conducts the show aimlessly, if not, indeed, malici-
> ously, that men and women run around automatically seeking
> escapes from their troubles and outlets for their lusts. The crowd

is still more incensed when an author who believes these things refuses to write about them seriously.

In many of his books Van Vechten has his characters speak for their author's critical judgments and literary tastes, but in *Firecrackers* he sets the stage on a number of occasions for Gareth Johns to explain Van Vechten's working creed as a novelist. At one point Johns delivers his pronouncement on method:

> ... you must think of a group of people in terms of a packet of firecrackers. You ignite the first cracker and the flash fires the fuse of the second, and so on, until, after a series of crackling detonations, the whole bunch has exploded, and nothing survives but a few torn and scattered bits of paper, blackened with powder.

The book which announces this technique in its title suggests a curious relation to the musical fantasy "Fireworks," an early composition of Igor Stravinsky, the Russian exponent of exciting rhythms and strange, discordant harmonies, whose new music had struck Van Vechten's ear so forcibly and favorably in his years as a music critic. Discussing this composition, Van Vechten had written, "No doubt Strawinsky's *Fireworks* would make a nice blaze without the name but the title gives us a picture to begin with." The statement is equally applicable to the novel. Stravinsky's fantasy begins with a rather fast, rhythmical step, moves into a deeper, more thoughtful sequence, then concludes with two or three crescendos in a series of chromatic arpeggios, advancing and declining octaves. The pattern of the novel is similar.

Into the society of Campaspe Lorillard, Paul Moody, and their coterie of cultivated clowns comes the disrupting riddle of the fabulous Gunnar O'Grady, an attractive youth with a remarkable personal history and philosophical bent. Gracefully, if unwittingly, Gunnar eludes their search for him through New York, appearing only long enough to revive the curiosity of his seekers. That these appearances reveal him as a furnaceman with a book of Persian poetry, a salesman in a flower shop, a pantomimist in the window display of a clothing store, and a professional acrobat, is some indication of his character.

It is Paul Moody who first discovers and explores the compelling force of Gunnar O'Grady, but it is the marvelously detached Campaspe who meets it head-on with her own personal power. The mystic strength of Gunnar's personality endows him with a disturbing aura of appeal that appears to others, on occasions of emanation, disturbingly suggestive of a halo. Everybody loves him but nobody can understand him. They recognize only that his mysterious appeal and his disturbing concern for their welfare comes from some inner peace and elemental goodness. Paul, probing at its source through the lad's benevolent double-talk, almost blunders into it at one point: "Do you understand any better?" asks O'Grady. "I'll be damned if I do," answers Paul, "but it doesn't matter. It's interesting enough without understanding." Gunnar hints at its accuracy only by tears glistening in the corners of his eyes.

With Campaspe, however, Gunnar can maintain no such aloof benevolence. There grows between the two a field subject to the stress and pull of two powerful magnets, opposite poles creating a mutual attraction which can cease only when the weaker submits to the pull of the stronger. Campaspe, although her superiority is in jeopardy, wins, the wretched O'Grady yielding himself to her pull, fatal in its effect on his course. Campaspe, composed again, offers herself only with the condescension of the victor who has proved superiority, and in the process has lost any need for the fruits of desire.

Campaspe's temporary doubts about her otherwise perfect balance are reminiscent of a remark of Van Vechten's recollected in the memoirs of Mabel Dodge Luhan: " 'Do you know what love is?' Carl asked of me one day. . . . 'It is to feel the way a kitten feels when a man holds it high up in the air in the palm of his hand.' " Mrs. Luhan adds, "I don't know whether he meant the kitten didn't know enough to be scared of falling, or whether it knew with panic the man would let it down." The detachment of a cat, not the dependence of a kitten, was Campaspe's goal.

The philosophy heard *sotto voce* in *Firecrackers* is disturbing and typical. It is selfish by most standards, putting the individual above the group in the quest for personal balance. It is a kind of sophisticated satanism. Campaspe is the proponent who must be on top of everyone and everything encountered in life.[6] Even in love, she must be able to deny herself her natural wishes, she must be superior to her lover, she must reassert her individual self-sufficiency, she must see her lover's subjugating need for her before she can retain that detached balance which is so necessary to her. Then she is free, while Gunnar, unable to cope with his desire in like manner, is damned. It is *Thaïs* with the modern dress and trappings of the Anatole France of New York. It is Adam and Eve, the temptation and the fall, with the innovations of arch fantasy. In her exclusive way, Campaspe is the dark angel who triumphs over the angel with the vulnerable halo, and her invincible individuality bests his sort of divinity.

Surrounding this fable is the entertaining scene of Van Vechten's New York, aspects of which are caught by no other author. Manhattan, he has asserted elsewhere, is too engrossing to leave for even a day. His pictures of the city, which serve every novel save *The Tattooed Countess* and *Spider Boy,* display a lively fascination in metropolitan animation. "For him," a friend observed, "Manhattan never loses its Arabian Nights glamor, and all the hanging gardens of Babylon are in its sky-line." Of the book, Louis Bromfield wrote, ". . . in Carl Van Vechten's 'Firecrackers' we found such a mirror of New York life, in a few of its many phases, as we have not yet encountered. . . . Mr. Van Vechten is not ponderous in his books, but he comes much nearer to depicting the American scene than many a laborious, cornfed realist."

In this same review was the observation that "Mr. Van Vechten surely grows more shrewd (with a shrewdness not in the least banal or

---

6. F. Scott Fitzgerald was one of many readers who preferred the Campaspe novels. After reading *Firecrackers,* he wrote Van Vechten (July 27, 1925) with his usual lack of attention to spelling: "With the *Blind Bow Boy* I like it best of your four novels—it seems to me that this rather than *The Tatoed Countess* is your true line of genius—in Campaspe for example you suggest so much more than you say—she is the embodiment of New York, mysterious and delecate and entirely original, while Countess Natorini for all the amazing and virtuostic details about her past was really a 'character.' "

or transparent), and in *Firecrackers* he displays a new and impressive strength in the death of Ella Nattatorrini." W. Somerset Maugham, writing Van Vechten on August 13, 1925, expressed a similar judgment: "I was delighted to resume my acquaintance with your wonderful countess and I think her deathbed is one of the best bits of ironic writing that I have ever read." It is satisfying to find such recognition for the interpolated scene in which the half-delirious and dying Countess frantically attempts to overcome the ravages of sickness and old age in what proves to be the vain hope that the holy father arriving to render her last rites will be a young priest. It is a scene of "impressive strength," but it was not new; it was the strength of ironic tragedy felt for Lennie Colman, Ella's maiden sister, Lou Poore, and Ella Poore Nattatorrini herself in *The Tattooed Countess*. What *Firecrackers* lacked, except for this attached interlude, was the force and depth of imaginative realization which made characters, situations, and their ironic handling so memorable in Van Vechten at his best. He had proven that his method could tread successfully the middle ground between melange and melodrama. *Firecrackers* was a retreat towards the former.

8. *ON THE EVENING OF MARCH 30, 1914,* Van Vechten witnessed a New York production of Ridgely Torrence's *Granny Maumee,* an early attempt to portray the Negro from his own point of view. "Immediately," he later wrote, "I was seized with the idea of founding a real Negro theatre, in which Negroes should act in real Negro plays." Twelve years later, as the author of *Nigger Heaven,* he carried the idea into fiction.

There was a good deal in the background of the writer to bring such a book into being. His father had helped found a school for Negroes. At least two of his favorite authors had written of Negroes: Gertrude Stein in "Melanctha" of *Three Lives,* and Ronald Firbank in *Prancing Nigger.* Personal acquaintance had made him an intimate friend of the Negro world of Harlem and New York City. Before World War I he began developing an interest in, and knowledge of, Harlem, with Van Vechten going to Harlem and Harlem coming to the Van Vechten apartment, and his Negro friends accompanied him everywhere. He read widely in the works of Negro writers: Charles W. Chesnutt, James Weldon Johnson, Claude McKay, W. E. B. Du Bois, Jessie Fauset, Jean Toomer, Langston Hughes, and others both old and new.

In all his experience with the American Negro, Van Vechten found evidence of an amazing culture full-blown in the contrasts of its extremes, already distinct in its character and accomplishment, yet struggling in a white world to *be* what it had already become. He recognized the striking anomaly of a Harlem in America, and he saw no reason to ignore its presence. As a part of the American scene, Harlem made much of its competition pale and dreary. Widely known was its sensational element of raw existence and vice, but virtually unknown was the presence in Harlem of a sensitive, intellectual search for stability. That intelligent humanity had any place in American Negro life was difficult for the average American to believe. Misconceptions and partial knowledge separated Harlem from the United States in the national mind. Most Americans could draw only upon the record of passion and violence that comprised the folklore conception of Harlem; they had no way to complete the picture. A book which would reproduce the sprawl of Harlem, with accurate representation allotted to the diverse segments of its society, needed to be written.

Such a book demanded a writer who could speak without condescension, who could weave coherent patterns from the tremendous contrasts in persons and scenes to be discovered in Harlem life. To be an honest representation, and to reach the very audience whose misconceptions it meant to alter, it had to offer the colors, sensations, and passions of Harlem in the proportions actually present. Carl Van Vechten was its man. Joseph Hergesheimer's tribute in a letter to Van Vechten shortly after the book's publication indicates the success of this method: "Nigger Heaven is really an objective novel, a thing so rare as to be unique. This is specially a generation of easy autobiography, novels now are hardly more than shapeless collections of personal and irrelevant ideas and prejudices. . . . You have taken the simplest arrangement possible, the oldest and perhaps most valid of the stories, and made it absolutely serve your purpose. This it appears to me, is the most that can be done."

Nigger Heaven is part sociological tract, part intellectual history, part aesthetic anthropology, but it is all novel. Van Vechten was well aware of the possibility that such a compound might explode on contact with the air of prejudice which polluted the American atmosphere. He asked Alfred Knopf, his publisher, to give the book a long and careful build-up:

> Ordinarily . . . books should not be advertised so long in advance, but this book is different. It is necessary to prepare the mind not only of my own public, but of the new public which this book may possibly reach, particularly that public which lies outside New York. If they see the title, they will ask questions, or read 'The New Negro' or something, so that the kind of life I am writing about will not come as an actual shock.

To assure the authenticity of his treatment of Negro life and character, he studied and collected, at first- and secondhand, a mass of documentary material which, augmented considerably since, was the basis of the James Weldon Johnson Collection of Negro Arts and Letters established by Van Vechten at the Yale University Library. He prepared his book with care and caution. As a final check he submitted the manuscript to Johnson and to Negro author Rudolph Fisher before publication. But, as James Branch Cabell foresaw when he wrote Van Vechten on August 15, 1926, "I hopefully await the row this book must almost inevitably arouse in all camps," the explosion took place anyway.

On both sides of the imaginary fence at 110th street, which Van Vechten had hoped to whittle down, controversy raged. Generally, the white critic was favorable, the Negro critic, to Van Vechten's dismay, adverse, although there was disagreement on all sides. The extremes of the white reaction are represented by the sour, unqualified opinion of D. H. Lawrence: "It is a false book by an author who lingers in nigger cabarets hoping to heaven to pick up something to write about and make a sensation—and, of course, money"; and Ellen Glasgow's decision in *Bookman* that "the roots of this book cling below the shallow surface of sophistication in some rich soil of humanity. . . . That the book attempts to prove nothing, that it does not masquerade as ethnology in the fancy dress of a novel, that it points no moral and preaches no doctrine of equality—this absence of prophetic gesture makes 'Nigger Heaven' only the more impressive as a sincere interpretation of life." Eric Walrond saw the novel in proper perspective when he wrote for the *Saturday Review of Literature:* " 'Nigger Heaven' will be pointed to as a frontier work of an enduring order. As literature with a strong social bias it prepares the way for examination of the fruits of a cultural flowering among the Negroes which is now about to emerge."

Among the Negroes, James Weldon Johnson, Alice Dunbar Nelson, and George S. Schuyler were the only reviewers who approved the novel without reservation. Johnson, who wrote in his autobiography, "From the first, my belief had held that *Nigger Heaven* is a fine novel," certified the fulfillment of the author's purpose in his *Opportunity* review: "[He has] taken the material [Harlem] had offered him and achieved the most revealing, significant and powerful novel based on Negro life yet written. . . . The author pays colored people the rare tribute of writing about them as people rather than puppets." It is clear that the title of the book alienated many Negroes—particularly those who did not read it. Langston Hughes suggests that the readers in Harlem missed the irony of Harlem seen as a "segregated gallery in a theater, the only place where Negroes could see or stage their own show," and points out that Van Vechten certainly had been more fair to the Harlemites than he had been to his home folks in *The Tattooed Countess.* If Negroes failed to catch the irony implicit in the title, Van Vechten's careful preparation of the novel was vain on still another count, for he had allowed Byron Kasson to explicate the title in one of his carefully high-lighted speeches:

> Nigger Heaven! That's what Harlem is. We sit in our places in the gallery of this New York theatre and watch the

white world sitting down below in the good seats in the orchestra. Occasionally they turn their faces up towards us, their hard, cruel faces, to laugh or sneer, but they never beckon. It never seems to occur to them that Nigger Heaven is crowded, that there isn't another seat, that something has to be done.

It is clear now that those who rejected the novel did so for reasons or prejudices not inherent in the book itself. By 1930, when John Chamberlain surveyed the accomplishments of the Negro in literature for *Bookman*, it was evident that *Nigger Heaven* had largely fulfilled its purposes:

> The Negro may count himself fortunate that the success of *Nigger Heaven* helped to carry the publishers' forts for much of his work. [It] gave a powerful impetus to the novelists of Harlem; and in spite of its elements of tacked-on sophistication it succeeds in its own right, for its technique—the old wheel-technique of George Eliot—is skilful, and it is evidently close enough to the truth to receive the compliment of imitation by Negroes.

Since then, Van Vechten's work with American Negroes has left no doubt of his sincerity and service. The 1951 reprint of *Nigger Heaven* in an Avon pocket-size edition testifies to the lasting influence and value of the book.

In his special note for this edition, Van Vechten has summarized his plot as "one of the oldest stories in the world, the story of the Prodigal Son, without the happy ending of that Biblical history. In my book a boy from a small town is bewitched, bothered, and bewildered by a big time Lady of Pleasure and is unable to meet the demands made on his character by life in a big city." In the course of this conflict, not only the face but also the mind of Harlem is explored. *Nigger Heaven* is broadside in approaching its subject without sacrificing depth of characterization. The revelation of the prodigal Byron Kasson; the sensitive, tragically proud Mary Love; the queen of pleasure, Lasca Sartoris; the "Scarlet

Creeper," Anatole Longfellow; and many another minor character is provocative, complex, and considerable.[7]

The artistic presentation of extremes in Harlem life is balanced and consistent. Opening and closing in the dissolute atmosphere of a Harlem cabaret, it ranges to serious discussions, never artificially staged, of the color problem. One of these, as credible and intelligent today as it was in 1926, involves two young couples in a Harlem apartment shared by the two girls. Its climax is symbolic of the book's tragic temper. Tiring of the circles into which such a discussion inevitably is led, Van Vechten has them turn for release and relief to a phonograph record of Clara Smith. He then reproduces five lines of the blues, "Nobody knows duh way Ah feel dis mornin'..." If, as Langston Hughes has said, Van Vechten wrote "sympathetically and amusingly and well about a whole rainbow of life above 110th Street that had never before been put into the color of words," it should be added that the violet end of the spectrum was well represented.

9. *A CONSISTENT PATTERN* of alternation between ironic tragedy and ironic comedy runs through Carl Van Vechten's seven novels. *Peter Whiffle,* the only one which fits its category loosely, was followed by the light antics of *The Blind Bow-Boy; The Tattooed Countess* was given the confection of *Firecrackers* as dessert; after *Nigger Heaven* came the gay spoofing of Hollywood in *Spider Boy;* and *Parties,* in its way the most tragic of them all, concluded the sequence.

The comic relief Van Vechten supplied after his Harlem drama was the lightest of them all. The gaily colored balloons of the "Campaspe novels" were inflated with New York air; but into *Spider Boy* he

---

7. Among the characterizations is a memorable glimpse of H. L. Mencken, introduced as Russett Durwood, the young editor of the "American Mars." Reminiscing about his friend, Van Vechten has since written, "I have tried to sketch a portrait of him in my novel *Nigger Heaven,* but it is almost impossible to capture his personality in a few brief paragraphs."

put the helium of Hollywood. His 1928 balloon flew high, but not blind. Van Vechten had been to Hollywood in the winter of 1926-1927. He saw a good deal of the Fitzgeralds who lived in an adjoining bungalow of the Ambassador. He made the acquaintance of many of the film stars, including Greta Garbo, and formed more intimate friendships with Aileen Pringle, Carmel Myers, and Lois Moran. While he didn't work in Hollywood, he did familiarize himself with the industry, the colony, and its people. In 1927, four Van Vechten articles on the film capital made a tandem appearance in *Vanity Fair* as a result of this visit and as a prelude to *Spider Boy:* "Fabulous Hollywood," "Hollywood Parties," "Hollywood Royalty," and "Understanding Hollywood." He had absorbed with amusement the peculiarities that set Hollywood apart from the rest of the world. It was fitting, then, that everything in *Spider Boy* took on size without gaining stature.

The novel opens with the presentation of a New York-bred situation that had the whimsical stamp of Van Vechten's irony. Ambrose Deacon, already a successful, comfortable, but little known writer, has been hailed as a new literary genius because of his highly successful first play, written without pretense or self-conscious art. On this account he has been besieged by critics, intellectual admirers, and the press in quest of his method, his artistic creeds, his techniques of form and style. As a consequence, the utterly ingenuous Ambrose becomes so self-conscious he can no longer write. Like the Countess Nattatorrini, Ambrose Deacon is leaving the scene of his discomfort in the hope that simpler, more peaceful surroundings will renew his spirits and his balance. As in *The Tattooed Countess,* the narration is begun on a train moving westward across America, but unlike that novel, the farther from New York it moves the less it fulfills the promise of its opening; for the innocent Ambrose, on his way to the rough adobe home of a friend in Santa Fe, encounters a mad group of movie folk on his train and is unwillingly whisked to the plaster palaces of Hollywood. The hilarity which ensues is an extravagant satire on the kingdom of the movies in the year 1928.

The first (almost the only) resident (there are no natives) of that realm who does not take Hollywood seriously is Capa Nolin, a girl writer.

In the sketch of her environment which she gives the meek, astonished Ambrose, she outlines in brief the subject, the type, and the manner of the book's satire: "... most of the houses out here are made of stucco. You can kick your foot right through them. You can kick your foot right through everything else here too. Nothing is real, except the police dogs and the automobiles, and usually those aren't paid for. To be concrete, there are no stenographers at the studios: they're all *secretaries*." In regard to sexual transgressions, the comedy is tastefully circumspect, lampooning the self-conscious amours of the promiscuous colony, but never stooping to record the earthy details. Ambrose Deacon, like the perpetual male fugitive of Thorne Smith's alcoholic novels, is pursued to his constant dismay by females, desirous of alliance with his name, talent, or influence; but he is eventually caught by Wilhelmina Ford, who, while she could not be judged normal (no one in *Spider Boy* is normal), is attracted to him for reasons of a less selfish nature.

A comparatively sane interlude in New Mexico, occasioned by Deacon's temporary escape from the egocentric society of Hollywood, graces the novel by sliding casually, although inconsistently, into the middle of the tale. By arriving thus briefly in Santa Fe, the book manages to inject some of the color of New Mexico scenes which Van Vechten has seen and photographed so memorably during his own visits there. The adobe home of Jack Story, the friend of Ambrose Deacon, probably was conditioned by Mabel Dodge Luhan's house in Taos, with its flock of white pigeons wheeling around outside, and its interior details of vigas overhead and objects of Indian and Spanish art placed about. A visit by Ambrose to an Indian pueblo is presented with respect visible beneath the comic turn of its prose. One almost wishes that Ambrose Deacon had taken a later train out of New York so that his tale could have been told in the setting of its original destination.

Spider Boy is good fun, however, and the reviewers who tossed it aside with heavy contempt missed the humorous twist of its double-tongued subtitle, "A Scenario for a Motion Picture." Clifton Fadiman was the most outspoken of these. His summary for *Bookman* read in part: "His satire is without sparkle or good nature and is so obvious that the attentive reader . . . scents it twenty pages ahead. On the whole, Mr. Van Vechten is a mediocre reporter of the smart cracks of five years ago and a fairly good purveyor to the appetites of upper-class fourteen-year-olds." The reviewer for the *London Times Literary Supplement* was another who ignored the parody in Van Vechten's book: "There are passages in this new novel of his in which he descends to rather wanton farce, moments in which his humor is of precisely the slapstick variety favoured by Hollywood." In addition to misinterpreting the author's satirical method, these readers deprived themselves of a good time by insisting on taking the novel seriously. Its author, within the rather flexible limits of his irony, didn't. Certainly its characters didn't. Its finale, while promising a more substantial volume should there be a sequel, tossed off the book it concluded with an impudence that characterized the whole project. Wilhelmina, done with Hollywood, rejected Ambrose's suggestion that they leave crowds, success, and fame, and retire together to a peaceful Cambodia. They were going to New York, the ex-Kansas girl declared: "I want to meet George Gershwin and Jimmy Walker and Percy Hammond and Mencken and Alfred Lunt and Theodore Dreiser and Fred Astaire and Carl Van Vechten and Paul Robeson and Scott Fitzgerald and Gene Tunney and . . . Cambodia! Why, we might as well live in Kansas City."

10. IF F. SCOTT FITZGERALD'S *This Side of Paradise* served as a literary overture to the "Roaring Twenties," Carl Van Vechten's last novel, *Parties* (1930), was even more clearly its coda. The place of the latter in a literary history of the decade is the more secure for the conscious purpose of its author. Fitzgerald was not aware at the time that he had provided a bible of flaming youth. Van Vechten was fully aware that he was conducting a wake, both for the giddy era and for his own gay cycle of novels. A special irony arises from the fact that David and Rilda Westlake, the central characters of Van Vechten's book, are based partly, according to its author, on Scott and Zelda Fitzgerald. In chronicling the alcoholic revolution of their dizzy, tragic merry-go-round existence, he succeeded in capturing the comic but grotesque spectacle of a bewildered society dancing at its own funeral, while his own demeanor as its literary choreographer was sobered by the realization that it was a closing performance. "It's just like the opening chorus of an opera bouffe," one of the characters remarks gaily at the impromptu morning cocktail gathering which concludes *Parties,* "all of us here clinking glasses like villagers on the green." "Somehow its more like the closing chorus," retorts another. "I think we're all a little tired."

Van Vechten's sense of form and proportion is as effective in *Parties* as it is in *The Tattooed Countess.* Its sputtering, bewildered, semi-coherent first three chapters are a sparkling representation of a drunken New York society, living from moment to moment and from drink to drink, not knowing quite what had happened, what was happening, or what would happen, but keeping the glitter and glibness of the immediate present forever animated. In the center of the novel is placed the only sober dialogue of any length, taking place quite properly against the backdrop of sunlight illuminating the apartment of David and Rilda Westlake. This sophisticated but explosively matched couple is allowed to pause in the light of noon before they plunge back into their frenetic existence. David delivers himself of virtually the whole theme and plot of the novel in one outburst:

> We're swine, filthy swine, and we are Japanese mice, and we are polar bears walking from one end of our cage to the other, to and fro, to and fro, all day, all week, all month, for ever to eternity. We'll be drunk pretty soon and then I'll be off to Donald's to get drunker and you'll be off with Siegfried and get drunker and we'll go to a lot of cocktail parties and then we'll all turn up for dinner at Rosalie's where you are never invited. She won't want you, and I shall hate you, but Siegfried will want you. And we'll get drunker and drunker and drift about night clubs so drunk that we won't know where we are, and then we'll

go to Harlem and stay up all night and go to bed late tomorrow morning and wake up and begin it all over again.

Parties, sighed Rilda. Parties!

From this occasion of disturbing illumination, the characters return to the alcoholic carrousel, the perpetual circle of which restores their customary moral vertigo. The ride is interrupted by a moment of moral judgment a second time, when a clairvoyant Negro woman, hired to entertain at a party, gives each member of the company (except the elusive David and Rilda) a reading, brief but direct, of his soul. Her portraiture too accurate, she is dismissed summarily before her revelations can be completed.

Parties is the only one of Van Vechten's novels which does not go anywhere. It concludes where it began, concluding nothing but the memorable exposition of scene, character, and atmosphere. The narrative is diverting and compelling throughout, but, save for the death of Roy Fern, a minor character with major attachments, and its consequences, there is no "working-out"; nothing is, in the usual sense, accomplished. This is perhaps the most consistent feature and reveals as much about the subject of the book as any technique could. To this strange timelessness, the sameness of scene, the drunken ride during which the changing view revolves but never alters, is added a sense of anomalous anachronism, subtly carried from the prophetic chaos of the early chapters to the later action of the book. The most striking instance of this is the disordered prophecy and fulfillment surrounding the death of Roy Fern, the bootlegger's flunky, fatally addicted to cocaine. In the incoherent hysteria of the opening pages, David Westlake cries, "I've killed a man or a man has killed me. There were three of us on the stairs. I mean ... O God!" Donald Bliss, the boy's employer, calls later to report, fallaciously, that Roy Fern had been killed. This prophecy, appropriately distorted through alcoholic visions, is fulfilled in Chapter Fourteen when Roy, drugged and deluded that he is defending David, stabs a rival and plunges down the stairs to his death in his wild attempt to escape.

Characters in the novel are extravagant and memorable. David and Rilda are supported by a vivid cast of dipsomaniacs: Bliss, the handsome bootlegger, and Roy, the snowbird; Beauty Butcher, the speakeasy pianist, and Simone Fly resembling "a gay Death," who was given to adding inane contributions to conversations, dropping liquor-filled glasses, and emitting as her perpetual expletive, "Blaaa!" There is Hamish Wilding whose sobering concern for David and Rilda luckily allows him to report the antics of others too drunk to report for themselves. The foreign element is represented by Noma Ridge, "a young English girl with dimpled, rosy cheeks who did not drink or smoke, but who atoned for the lack of these semi-precious vices by describing in an endless monotone the various forms of her amorous transports and the characteristics of the persons with whom she enjoyed them," and the aged Gräfin von Pulmernl und Stilzernl, who finds calm Old World pleasure in the frantic perversions of America. This distance qualifies her to deliver the final irony when she brings the book to its close, chuckling, "It is so funny, David, so very funny, and I love your country."

The last character to be introduced is the neglected eight-year-old son of David and Rilda. The child's name, through no chance we can be sure, is Regent. Someone had to take care of things until his parents grew up.

It is interesting to note in Van Vechten's final novel the tendency to return in some portions to the earlier style and manner of his essays. Some chapters begin with three or four pages of exposition devoted to an appropriate theme—the rapid, continuous mutations of New York City, or the colorful "Lindy Hop" ("Of all the dances yet originated by the American Negro, this the most nearly approaches the sensation of religious ecstasy") —before they pick up the hectic narrative again. This device has a genuinely warming effect on a novel that otherwise relies on the false heat generated by alcoholic intoxication. In addition, it allows the reader to separate the author from the ephemeral futility of the scenes he portrayed, a process which Carl Van Vechten, in the most morally inclined of his ironic tragedies, clearly recognized as inevitable and necessary.

Oddly enough, the critics displayed less understanding of Van Vechten's purposes and methods in *Parties* than they had for those in any of his other novels. Most reviewers, for reasons difficult to imagine, ignored its moral implications, possibly because, while moral questions were manifest to the author throughout the book, the author was never self-conscious about presenting them as didactic disquisitions. Some readers, like Fanny Butcher of the *Chicago Tribune*, merely expressed general disappointment: " 'Parties,' " she wrote, "is, to this reader's mind, the least of the works of Mr. Van Vechten." Harry Hansen, concerned only with the surface froth, wrote in the *New York World*, "Parties is in his best manner, free from the seriousness of Nigger Heaven, reminiscent of The Blind Bow Boy and The Tattooed Countess." Others lamented with Clinton Simpson, who reported on the book for the *Saturday Review of Literature*, "that he uses his talents for books such as this one, which is flippant at best and occasionally a little—even more than a little—cheap."

The most myopic and unkind of all was the reviewer for the *New York Times*, who, blithely disregarding the years and events which separated *Peter Whiffle* and *Parties* as well as missing the moral tragedy in the novel, wrote, "A book as unsavory and sniggering as it is dull. It is something of a shock that a man so well acquainted with the arts as Mr. Van Vechten should so far have forgotten himself as to spin out this tasteless and specious tale." Perhaps this reception of *Parties* was an appropriately ironic climax to Van Vechten's career as a novelist. In any event, today it appears indicative of the reluctance with which the generation of the Twenties viewed itself at the end of the era.

With *Parties*, the series of seven novels in nine years was completed. Individually, they had been sources of amusement, novelty, edification, shock, and sophistication to a decade that constantly sought these qualities in both life and literature. Collectively, as George Dangerfield has observed, they constitute a comedy of manners for their accelerated era. *Parties* demonstrated that the same fate which befell the eighteenth-century comedy of manners also acted upon that of the Twenties: excesses from within brought a change from the unmoral to the moral.

and the Twenties 97

The philosophy of composition which is found in the series was symbolized in the title of its middle member, *Firecrackers*. Following the method explained by Gareth Johns in that book, all seven novels may be quickly appraised. *Peter Whiffle*, with its variety of effects, comes closest to the colorful displays of a professional pyrotechnician. *The Blind Bow-Boy*, *Firecrackers*, and *Spider Boy*, lacking the substance and impact of the others, go off like a hopping string of explosions. *The Tattooed Countess*, *Nigger Heaven*, and *Parties*, with the added preparation, suspense, and heightened effect of cannon crackers, sizzle and spark enticingly before going off with a report loud and singular enough to rebound echoes for some time to come.

IV. SOCIETY:

The Circus and the Sideshows

A THIRTY-MAN SYMPOSIUM was published in 1922 under the ambitious title, *Civilization in the United States.* Its table of contents broke the title into thirty segments, each represented by an individual essay and an individual author. The subjects were The City, Politics, Journalism, The Law, Education, Scholarship and Criticism, School and College Life, The Intellectual Life, Science, Philosophy, The Literary Life, Music, Poetry, Art, The Theatre, Economic Opinion, Radicalism, The Small Town, History, Sex, The Family, The Alien, Racial Minorities, Advertising, Business, Engineering, Nerves, Medicine, Sport and Play, and Humour. Representative contributors to the symposium were Lewis Mumford, H. L. Mencken, John Macy, Robert Morss Lovett, Joel Spingarn, Harold Stearns (also the editor), Van Wyck Brooks, Deems Taylor, Conrad Aiken, George Jean Nathan, Hendrik Van Loon, Elsie Clews Parsons and Ring Lardner. Together, their survey of America was disturbing and significant. Their essays struggled for objectivity but could not remain dispassionate. They maintained hope and faith but they seldom were satisfied with the American life they discussed. They somehow fell short of evoking the whole, but that is to be expected, for most authors reflect themselves as much as their scene.

Oddly, the table of contents comes closer to presenting a unified picture than do the essays. The thirty components of "civilization" include some that would be out of place in any other period. Earlier eras might have added The City, Journalism, Radicalism, The Small Town, and The Family to the traditional list, but what other age would have

Fania Marinoff and her Husband, Carl Van Vechten
as photographed on May 21, 1930, by Nickolas Muray

given equal billing to Sex, Racial Minorities, Advertising, Nerves, Sport and Play, and Humour?

The contents tell us something else of the Twenties, for listed there are names of many of those, some in youth, some in middle age at the time, who led the intellectual revolt from tradition that opened the way for the era's most remarkable achievements and its most irresponsible failures, and endowed the decade with its unique personality.

1. IN HIS TRAINING, his sympathies, his intellectual convictions and his personal environment, Carl Van Vechten was identified with this group. Indeed, he was intimately acquainted with most of its members. He was a personal and professional friend of Mencken, Nathan, Lovett, Taylor, Spingarn, Macy, and Stearns, to mention only a sampling. As a persistent habitué of the salons, social gatherings, intellectual haunts, and parties of New York, London, and Paris, he held an acquaintance among the cosmopolitan intelligentsia of his time that few could equal. Himself an exponent of experimentalism in art and aesthetic bohemia in living, he moved in the company of those intellectually and artistically dedicated to the assertion of individual expression in the face of tradition. And he moved more comfortably than most.

Oscar Cargill, in his history of intellectual America, has written that "Carl Van Vechten belongs to the Intelligentsia by his undiscriminating eclecticism, more than for any other reason. It has made his career as an intellectual peculiarly pointless, which result the clan generally applauds as the highest merit in its membership." With the caution that "undiscriminating" is not to be read as "indiscriminate," the estimate is true; but it is a surface truth. It forgets that the human comedy can sometimes be seen most pointedly as comedy.

Peter Whiffle is the best answer to the charge of pointless eclecticism, but it is not alone. Most of Van Vechten's work both as essayist and novelist, points, sometimes unconsciously but more often purposely, to the scenes, the ideas, the personalities, the ironic paradoxes that only such an eclectic adventurer could collect and record. It is the spirit of an inveterate collector that infuses the work of Van Vechten with purpose, for he has collected and presented in his books a potpourri of his own life and times: personal collections of portraits, rare prints, handbills, diaries, program notes, manifestoes, caricatures, invitation lists, social notes, creeds, recipes, enchantments and their antidotes, menus, panaceas, picture post cards, and comic valentines, more illuminating in their diversity than any single-minded study could be. If he was the butterfly of his society instead of its gadfly, it merely meant that he was more socially acceptable; he goaded less and was allowed to observe more. If his eclectic method seemed inconsistent in a society of individuals given to narrower self-dedication, it assumed the larger purpose of absorbing the contrasts within that same society. Such concern for consistency, Van Vechten agreed with Emerson, was the hobgoblin of little minds; in addition, it had the trappings of tradition.

Van Vechten's most valuable asset as a commentator on his scene was his ability to identify himself with the society in which he moved, while at the same time remaining an interested, detached observer of its performances. He was a singular example of the one-man show; besides being one of the actors on stage, he was also occasionally its director, and at all times its audience. His motive, consistent with the mood of the time, was an escape from boredom in the pursuit of novelty and amusement. Unlike so many restless souls in the Twenties, he found it and captured it in the very comedy of the chase.

2. THE CRITICAL UNREST and intellectual wanderlust that served as a prelude to the Twenties is present in Van Vechten's early work. His critical essays on music and the arts establish his place in the revolt of the young intellectuals. In anticipation of Mencken and his henchmen, he could declare, "The ironclad dreadnoughts of the academic world, the reactionary artists, the dry-as-dust lecturers are constantly ignoring the most vital, the most real, the most important artists while they sing polyphonic, antiphonal, palestrinian motets in praise of men who have learned to imitate comfortably and efficiently the work of their predecessors." Peter Whiffle echoed the sense of intellectual isolation that made the sensitive individual an uneasy, inarticulate prophet in the Waste Land. Like T. S. Eliot's frustrated Prufrock, Peter shook his head vainly at conventional answers to his questions: "I thought you would say that but that's not what I meant, that's not at all what I meant."

The scenes and atmosphere of Van Vechten's experience in Europe during the stormy months that saw the beginning of World War I are vividly recollected in his sensitive diary-essay, "July-August 1914." He was in Italy and France at the time, one of thousands of American tourists and self-exiled intellectuals living in the Continental dream of individual escape. His companions, Mabel Dodge,[1] her son, John Evans, Neith Hapgood and her children, and sundry personalities discouraged by the temporal difficulties of reality that threatened their dream, made a cosmopolitan society much like that of F. Scott Fitzgerald's haunting *Tender Is the Night*. The essay re-creates without effort the confusion, the petulance, the resentment, and the discomfort of sophistication at bay, caught and baffled in the turbulence of an insistent reality it thought it had escaped.

He celebrated the American's discovery of Paris, a trend that had turned that city into a mecca for the disillusioned and inhibited intellects of the United States. Americans crossed the Atlantic in unprecedented droves to experience what John Gould Fletcher has called "the greatest market and rag fair of culture and of international license in the world." The legends of dispossessed Americans on the Left Bank multiplied rapidly, and made the vision of an American in Paris grow more glamorous and inviting than ever. The old *Life* printed a cartoon during the postwar rise of Left Bank society which mocked the movement at the same time that it illustrated its appeal. Four alcoholic Americans are shown at a Montparnasse bar, flanked by copies of Hemingway's *The*

1. In all Van Vechten's work, Mabel Dodge (Luhan) is referred to as Edith Dale. This diary-like account allows one slip, however, when he writes of registering "a trunk for Mabel."

Sun Also Rises and Eugene Jolas's exile magazine, *transition*. "Garçon, what's that the orchestra's playing?" is the inquiry of one drunk. "Why that's the Star-Spangled Banner, sir," is the answer.

Readers who shared vicariously in the delights of discovering Paris were given their share of anecdotes and Parisian wares in the essays of Van Vechten, and could even assume his cosmopolitan air by agreeing with his observation that "We will never have a national music until we have national dishes and national drinks and until we like good food. It is significant that our national drinks at present are mixed drinks, the ingredients of which are foreign." But *Peter Whiffle* gave them even more than they had a right to expect. Besides offering Continental authenticity in its back-drops for the narrative, it interpolated whole passages devoted to the sophisticated scenes and personages of contemporary Paris. In the longest of these, the author gave five pages to events seen, places visited, occasions shared, personalities and celebrities viewed and met (including Olive Fremstad and the Steins), a casual catalogue of the cream of Parisian experiences. It was concluded by the nonchalant remark, "In short, you will observe that I did everything that young Americans do when they go to Paris."

More Americans have had the chance to visit Gertrude Stein because of Van Vechten than otherwise might have. Her autobiography states, "Carl Van Vechten has had a delightful habit all these years of giving letters of introduction to people who he thought would amuse Gertrude Stein. This he has done with so much discrimination that she has liked them all."

On the Continent, Van Vechten absorbed the extremes of society. His impressions of backstreet Paris are perpetuated in the colorful vignette, "Au Bal Musette," while *Peter Whiffle* transcribes some of the intellectual discussions of the international set in Italy and France. In his biography of John Reed, Granville Hicks sketches such an occasion when "Mabel Dodge's *jeunes gens assortis,* in Miss Stein's phrase," Reed, Robert Edmond Jones, and Van Vechten, were together in Florence with guests coming in evenings: "There were triangular arguments between Mrs. [Muriel] Draper, Jones, and Van Vechten about painting. Van

Vechten quarreled with Arthur Rubenstein and Mrs. Draper about Bach."

This association with Mabel Dodge, which she has described as "a long drawn-out friendship with ups and downs in it and a good deal of sympathy and anger alternating on my part," gave Van Vechten a box seat from which to witness the parade of the intelligentsia, the artists, the reformers, the iconoclasts, and the merely eccentric who passed through her fabulous salon. Her apartment at 23 Fifth Avenue in New York was the crossroads of our intellectual bohemia, and her villa at Florence extended its stage to international proportions. Van Vechten was an early member of her group and has remained an affectionate friend through a series of trials and misunderstandings. In the recollection of their first encounter, Mrs. Luhan has sketched in quick, deft strokes the personality he brought to her gatherings: "He seemed amused at everything; there wasn't a hint of boredom in him. 'A young soul,' I thought to myself in my superior way, as I smiled across at him. After dinner he sought me out and made gay, affectionate fun of the Armstrongs in an undertone.... He amused me because he had such a sense of humor and was so full of life."

While Mabel Dodge moves through many of Van Vechten's books, it is in *Peter Whiffle* that her famous New York salon is depicted. Max Eastman also suggested Mabel Dodge and her salon group in action in his novel, *Venture*, using the name "Mary Kittredge." In Van Vechten's presentation, the tone is not as serious as the occasion and the people present might have wished, but in keeping with the personality of the novel and its author, it is affectionate fun-making rather than serious satire. Having suggested to Peter that he include a chapter on Edith Dale's gatherings in his book, Carl blithely does it for him in the book of Peter's which, the reader has been told, Van Vechten is writing for him. The evening is reported with emphasis on the contrasting mixture of ideas and personalities, heavy and light, serious and silly, that animated the scene. It introduces talk on art consciousness by Max Weber, the violence of labor strikes by Bill Haywood, and snatches of conversations both heated and casual. "The groups separated, came together, separated, came together, separated, came together," it concluded: "Syndicalists, capitalists, revolutionists, anarchists, artists, writers, actresses, 'perfumed with botanical creams,' feminists, and malthusians were all mixed in this strange salad."

By the time Mabel Dodge had become weary of her service and amusement as hostess-patroness of the intelligentsia, and had left for a new colony and a new life in Taos, New Mexico, Van Vechten had established himself as a host to the New York set, a role he has continued to play with genial success through the endless search for parties in the Twenties and the more sober need for a gathering place in the Thirties and Forties. *Firecrackers* kept his readers informed of "Edith Dale" by noting Campaspe Lorillard's reflection, upon receiving a letter from her, that she "seemed content to remain indefinitely in the rambling, Spanish house she had built for herself on a plateau in New Mexico."

In that same novel he added a more decisive comment on the perversity, irony, and contradiction in a society which inspired dedicated individuals to devote their careers to causes. In a speech about the efficacy of preachers, professors, and reformers, Gunnar O'Grady exclaims, "Why Margaret Sanger has actually turned a great many people against birth-control, and William Jennings Bryan has probably interested a great many people in drinking, and John Roach Straton and John Sumner are excellent guides to the pseudo-vices, and the Republicans make men good Democrats, and the Democrats make men good Republicans." Entertained and amused and often sympathetically attracted by causes and their exponents, Van Vechten usually maintained a detached critical awareness of their excess and self-conscious consistency of purpose. Occasionally, this attitude led to a supercilious dismissal of anything that took definite form and character, but always it recognized the follies of a rigid point of view. An example of both is found in an assessment of contemporary literary criticism expressed in a letter to Emily Clark. Discussing work by a critic writing for the *Reviewer*, he predicted a brilliant future "when he begins to realize that the middle radicals and the young intellectuals and the ultra-virile adolescents and even the homosexuals are frequently just as silly (or even sillier) as (or than) Sherman and More."

3. THE TWENTIES in the United States produced an adolescent, imitation *decadence* that is peculiar in a historical sense. The word sits uneasily on the era, but it is nonetheless applicable to many aspects of its society. It featured contempt for the standards, morals, traditional restrictions on thought and conduct, and the sense of wholeness inherited from the past. It bred national neurosis and a dedication to the pleasures of the moment. It asserted individual freedom from cultural and moral taboos, and it fostered in art an inversion of the aesthetic which had previously demanded classic decorum, simplicity, order, and unity. It sought in art and life the ideal symbolized by Dionysus, an ideal related to both love and intoxication, either of which promises momentary ecstasy as its ultimate reward.

That it was not real decadence, that it was the product of impetuosity and revolt rather than of age and maturity, that its presence in the nation-at-large was never secure, all these observations are true, but they are also misleading. The generation that reflected postwar bohemia in its fads and philosophy was seldom aware that this was only a reflection. In the excesses of the Twenties, in the veneer of release and the inability to dispense with the conscience even while ignoring it, the era practiced willful self-deception. But in their more subtle modulations these same elements in our society led the nation to a new maturity and self-realization that would not have developed without the impetus of revolt and experiment. On the surface, the movement was one of running away, but within the headlong race was the motion of running toward.

Bohemianism (in the Twenties characteristically shortened to its adjective form) was the term used: perhaps *decadence* lacked the essential ring of modernity. "One moment of real life is worth a ton of platitudes (like the one I've just written)," was James Huneker's expression of it. Walter Lippmann puzzled over its impact on social philosophy: "The attempt to measure the degree in which impulse is to be permitted to express itself is obviously full of difficulties . . . . Morality, if it is not fixed by custom and authority, becomes a mere matter of taste determined by the idiosyncracies of the moralist." Some, like Ernest Boyd in an article published in Mencken's and Nathan's first issue of the *American Mer-*

cury, ridiculed with direct satire the pose, fraud, insufficiency, and unconscious hypocrisy of the aesthete of the early Twenties.

Van Vechten maintained a precarious balance. Bohemian himself by inclination and association, he wrote of people devoted to the uninhibited moment, but his affection for them did not prevent his exposure of their follies. Instead he made the amusing exposition of those follies the basis of his books. Peter Whiffle exhausted the possibilities of aesthetic realization and found himself, instead. The sophisticated characters of *The Blind Bow-Boy* and *Firecrackers* outdid each other in their attempts to banish boredom through perverse and novel pleasures, but over them reigned the detached super-sophisticate, Campaspe, whose more stable pleasure came not from her own participation, but from the detached observation of the others. "It was only . . . those who expected to find amusement in themselves who wandered about disconsolate and bored. Amusement was to be derived from watching others, when one permitted them to be entirely themselves."

Except for *Parties,* and, to a lesser extent the preceding novels, *Nigger Heaven* and *Spider Boy,* the line separating Van Vechten from the milieu of his characters is a tenuous one. Campaspe displays an awareness above that of her companions, but she is disturbingly unaffected and supreme in her lack of conscience. Her ego is admissable, but it is undisciplined by any super-ego. At best, it observes with aloofness what it chooses to call "comportment" rather than evoke the morality of the term "deportment." The reader is shocked not so much by the characters' immorality as he is by the author's unmorality. It was somehow insufficient to accept as the whole man Mabel Dodge Luhan's explanation that "With him amusing things were essential things; whimsicality was the note they must sound to have significance." With the last three novels, however, the balance was reaffirmed. Still picturing the excesses of bohemianism, *Nigger Heaven* made them the tools of a tragedy. *Spider Boy* applied its own antic disposition to the outlandish West Coast imitation of the real thing. *Parties,* at the end of the era, described the clientele of the Wishbone, the speakeasy in which harried, abandoned sophisticates clustered almost in mutual protection from reality, as cosmopolitan. "Perhaps bohemian—if one may revive a worn out epithet that once meant a great deal—" it added, "would be a more exact word."

4. *PUBLIC TASTE IN THE TWENTIES* worshipped at four altars: sophistication, popularity, modernity, and expediency. The first of these promised the social commodity known as "class," and put a premium on style and quality. The second provided safety in numbers and allowed the mass of America to maintain its respectability without appearing dated. The third made it necessary to keep *ahead* of the Joneses, and led to the succession of fads that kept the decade hopping from one interest to another. The fourth, in addition to reflecting the national inclination toward what was easy, was a question of financial and geographical availability, answered in full by the business skills of mass merchandising, distribution, and retail marketing.

Evidence of the popular move toward sophistication, toward "class," is found in both the cultural and the commercial life of the Twenties. At some levels, the war on pretentiousness and frippery was being successfully waged. American taste improved steadily in the pictorial arts during the Twenties. Simplicity and functionalism made rapid headway in the fields of architecture and design. Taste in the fine arts, the "lively" arts, and the domestic arts became more thoughtful, more sophisticated, and more cosmopolitan. But in almost all respects, American taste was guilty of overindulgence in its blind obeisance to one or more of these four altars.

Mature American readers acclaimed *The New Yorker*, started in 1925 by Harold Ross, for its animation, wit, and its unyielding war on pretentiousness. But at the same time, real estate agents, in an attempt to add "class" to their profession, became realtors, beauty operators became beauticians, undertakers became morticians, and even clerks became salespersons. The functional simplicity of modern design gave way in the popular mind to the stark angularity of modernistic lines. The urge to be "as modern as tomorrow" let the national taste assume that whatever was new was desirable. Modernity and the overnight acclaim that it bred for so many foundationless fads led away from real sophistication. Mass production assured popularity through standardization, while mass marketing encouraged the growth and continuation of poor taste by making its wares widely available and socially necessary.

In such a society, sophistication is easily lost in its own popular counterfeit, but it is no less desirable for that. The art of living comfortably and contentedly in the midst of one's accessories is sought by the many, but known only to the few. A regard and affection for these accessories reflecting pleasure *in the things themselves,* rather than reflecting extraneous motives for their possession, is even more rare.

To as fine a degree as anyone writing in America during the era, Joseph Hergesheimer and Carl Van Vechten utilized this epicurean art of taste and of charming living. Hergesheimer's novels were furnished by an author who knew what he liked and why he liked it. He delighted in the texture of fine fabrics, the tints of glassware, the grace of the craftsman's art in furniture, the bouquet of rare wines, and the exotic effects of exquisite jewelry. His was the art of sensuous refinement, antique in its flavor and consistently conscious of atmospheric essence.

The décor in Van Vechten's books was more lively, more variable, more personal, and more vulnerable to imitation than Hergesheimer's, but the personal sense of atmosphere was just as evident. Individuality was the keynote, and the reflection of its owner's personality was the creed. In an early essay, impudently entitled, "In Defense of Bad Taste," he had discussed the personal aspects of interior decoration, asserting that the selection of household items and bric-a-brac should be made by the individual rather than by a professional decorator. He ridiculed the prevalent methods represented by the typical American millionaire who spent a fortune on furnishings which served in no way his personality or individuality, only to discover he didn't like them and couldn't use them. In his novels, Van Vechten revealed characters through the self-expression (or the lack of it) to be found in their surroundings, in the furnishings they had chosen to live with. Peter Whiffle, of course, is the outstanding example; each new dedication to a way of life and a means to art in

Peter's restless career is signalled by a new abode and a new set of personal appurtenances. Only cats, Van Vechten's symbol of the philosophy which Peter gradually discovers as the goal of his quest, accompany Peter through all his settings. Gareth Johns and Lennie Colman in *The Tattooed Countess*, Mary Love in *Nigger Heaven*, and others are revealed, in a similar fashion, through the choice of their surroundings. Even Mrs. Alonzo W. Syreno, the unimaginative pretender among the weary sophisticates of *Parties*, employs an English decorator who gives her home the stamp of "a permanently uninhabited English house," and betrays her lack of both taste and imagination in its alien character.

It was inevitable that Van Vechten should reveal himself as well as his characters through this feature of his writing. His sense of rapport with objects and possessions is a part of all his work, disclosing through the catalogues of impedimenta and decorations his own taste for the exotic, the unusual, the colorful, and the sensuous.

Mabel Dodge Luhan has written of his ability to animate her surroundings through a sympathetic appreciation of them:

> He entered the exquisitely ordered and prepared apartment and he enjoyed it so much that he seemed to give it a gently vibrating awareness of itself. He never realized that the lovely objects all gathered together in a perfect pattern had no life of their own nor even any borrowed life from me, and he gave them such an appreciation of the cozy living world they made ... that there was an instant response from all those inanimate things and the place became alive for us and for all others who ever afterwards entered there. He set it going on its changing round of appearances.

To the few who followed the example of his tastes and manners as a means to self-cultivation, and as a method of achieving genuine pleasure through the personal development of artistic appreciation, Van Vechten brought the same animation as he had to Mabel Dodge. To the bulk of his readers, for whom he was an end product to be imitated, a curious model that one should, for some reason, pattern one's way after if sophistication was to be gained, he was another fad of the Twenties, the author to read, the thing to do, the pattern to follow, the means of keeping above (and ahead of) the next fellow—who was employing the same vain means to the same futile end.

5. *ANY AUTHOR* who indulged his whims and thrived on novelty was in tune with the Twenties. A society which immediately caught up anything novel, strange, or modern, and just as quickly dropped it for the next item in the series, could accept as its own the writer who was likely to discover some new field or exciting interest with each new book. In an age of fads, Van Vechten was one of the leading faddists. He introduced new composers, the emotions of the blues, Gertrude Stein, the Harlem vogue, strange and exotic figures in literature, and the lively performers of stage entertainments. To him the unusual experience was the most satisfying, although not necessarily the most lasting. "Life was perceived to be a fastidious circus," Mrs. Luhan recalls, "and strange conjunctions were more prized than the ordinary relationships rooted in eternity."

In his personal life he cultivated caprice and whimsy. He was amused by exhibitionism, sometimes his own as well as that of others. He turned whim into custom by having his signature on the contracts of all his books after 1920 witnessed by "someone in some way connected with the subject or the intention or the dedication of each book." Thus Fania Marinoff, the actress who became Mrs. Van Vechten, served for *Peter Whiffle*, Hugh Walpole for *The Blind Bow-Boy*, Theodore Dreiser for *The Tattooed Countess*, H. L. Mencken for *Excavations*, James Branch Cabell for *Firecrackers*, Sinclair Lewis (for the sake of the pun) for *Red*, James Weldon Johnson for *Nigger Heaven*, Charlie Chaplin (Van Vechten traveled across the continent to indulge this sentiment) for *Spider Boy*, Texas Guinan for *Parties*, and Eugene O'Neill for *Sacred and Profane Memories*.

In joining the national passion for novelties and fads, however, his disregard for confining consistency once again enabled him to participate in the amusements at the same time as he pointed out their ridiculous features. His novels consistently satirized the aberrations and characteristics of the same public that received them so enthusiastically. The antics that endeared American society to Van Vechten, and provided subjects for his novels, were shown to their perpetrators in the light of their pretentious foolishness, but were accepted more often than not as amusing caricatures of others. To Van Vechten this must have been the most grotesque, and therefore the most entertaining, twist of all. Much the same thing happened with Sinclair Lewis's satires of middle-class America, but there was tragedy in the readers' reluctance to identify the characters with themselves. For the satires of Carl Van Vechten, the situation served only to heighten the comedy.

In *Parties,* he employed the phrases and pet expressions of the time to the point of fine ridicule. "There's music to that" is the inevitable comment following the inadvertent use of a song title in conversation. Just as inevitable is its tired counter-reply, "I know." Simone Fly terminates her inane remarks with the unconscious pertinence of her "Blaaa." "We're here because we're here," mimics a character at the conclusion of the book, and Van Vechten has him add with not much more originality, "and we should be extremely silly not to make the worst of it." Ambrose Deacon, before he is set upon by the egomaniacs of Hollywood in *Spider Boy,* runs through the prescribed ritual of the times in the solitude of his train compartment: "He had read the current issue of the Saturday Evening Post to the last advertising page; he had considered the plight of the poor farmer; he had reflected on the subject of Calvin Coolidge; he had even wondered whether there was a God."

The craze for cults is lampooned in *Firecrackers* with the life story of Pinchon's Prophylactic Plan, conceived rather suddenly by Emmaline Pinchon, a governess at the time of inspiration. The plan was a philosophy of acrobatics which held as some of its principles, "Deep breathing while standing on the head during the simultaneous consideration of the ultimate oneness of God with human kind, the essential co-ordination of the waving left arm with the soul, and the identity of the somersault with the freedom of the will."

The Duke of Middlebottom, asserting that "Everything that one called modern a year ago [1922] is old-fashioned [in 1923]," gives quite a catalogue to "prove" his point. Among his items of modernity are Freud, Mary Garden, Einstein, Wyndham Lewis, Dada, glands, the Six, vers libre, radio, the Ziegfeld Follies, cubism, Sacha Guitry, Ezra Pound, The Little Review, vorticism, Marcel Proust, The Dial, uranians, Gordon Craig, prohibition, the young intellectuals, Sherwood Anderson, normalcy, Charlie Chaplin, fireless cookers, ectoplasm, the tango, and Negro dancing.

Perhaps the most direct portraiture of all, and the most double-barreled because it attended to both the celebrity-idolizing public and the hypocritical elite, was Lalla Draycott, introduced to the readers of *Firecrackers* for no other ostensible reason than to sketch an amusing type from the Twenties. She rode a black stallion in the park every morning. When it was possible and fashionable, she indulged in fox-hunting. "She attended football and baseball games, and race-meets, and played golf and tennis. She knew the names of every celebrity mentioned on the sporting pages of the newspapers. She could talk about Paavo Nurmi, Georges Carpentier, Jack Dempsey, Vincent Richards, or Epinard for an entire day without stopping . . . whereas it is doubtful if she knew whether Anatole France was President of the Swiss Republic or a member of the Irish Parliament. She went to all the prize-fights and wrestling-matches in Madison Square Garden, usually occupying ringside seats. She enjoyed a bowing acquaintance with Tex Rickard. No horse- or dog-show ever opened without her presence. She wore mannish suits and smoked little cigars especially made for her." Lalla Draycott was, in a phrase that can work two ways, no dream.

6. *ULICK INVERN*, the bohemian hero of James Huneker's 1920 novel, *Painted Veils*, found himself uncomfortably perched "on the jagged edge of ennui." Much of America shared his discomfort in the ensuing ten years, and sought every imaginable way to keep from going over the edge. "Everywhere there is evidence of the search for the thrill,"

wrote Van Vechten in 1915, "by the masses, by individuals; revolution, fast motoring, war, feminism, Jew baiting, Alfred Casella, aeroplaning, the Russian Ballet, are sign posts which point ways to those who lack the ingenuity to invent personal thrills or at least the capacity to enjoy them." These were thrills one could enjoy at first hand; there were others more popular because less dangerous. The average citizen was satisfied by the vicarious thrill of identifying himself with the glamor, the charm, the adventure, and the success of the Celebrated Name.

The game was particularly satisfying when the public could boldly assume an affectionate equality with the object of their worship. Sixty thousand fans in Yankee Stadium didn't merely watch George Herman Ruth earn his tremendous salary by hitting a baseball four hundred feet into the streets of the Bronx; they cheered him for the opportunity he gave them to enter the game with "C'mon, Babe, hit one for me!" and then to share in the glory and exultation when he came through with the home run. A hundred twenty million Americans didn't adulate Charles A. Lindbergh, a young pilot who flew alone from New York to Paris; they idolized the shy "Lindy," as one of their own—the kid next door who had given them the thrill of danger, who had gambled as they would have feared to gamble, but in winning had let them share the victory.

Every celebrity, whether his by-line was "I love you all," "I just did it for the wife and kids," or "I want to be alone," was a public trust, yielding dividends in reflected glory, glamor, and charm. The nation sought to escape humdrum existence by its interest in the exciting lives of others. The names and personalties of "stars" cannot be neglected in a history of the period without losing something essential to its spirit. A convincing example is the photograph in Geraldine Farrar's autobiography showing her embarkation on a concert tour following her Metropolitan Opera farewell performance. In it, a mob of admirers swarm around the observation car platform with pennants reading "Farrar," and a sign mounted on the rear of the platform proclaims:

NONE BUT YOU

GerryFlappers

The celebrities themselves upheld the mania, leading lives consistent with the demand for glamor, charm, and unpredictability. They were singular beings, most of them, whose responsibility to their public was to maintain their own independent talent and power. Like Michael Arlen's Princess Baba, they defined the universe in terms of their own accomplishments. The Princess, in one of Arlen's seasonably popular sophisticated romances, blithely disagrees with the remark that we are all as God has made us. "By no means," she replies, "for some people are charming and some are not, and what does God know of charm? It is dreadful to lie awake at nights thinking that God lacks charm. Yet the word is never so much as mentioned in the Bible."[2] It was a word the Twenties knew, and it was an inevitable word in any discussion of Carl Van Vechten's books.

He gave his readers Mary Garden and Geraldine Farrar and Ronald Firbank and Elinor Wylie and Edith Dale and Peter Whiffle and Zimbule O'Grady and Campaspe Lorillard and Ella Nattatorrini and Gunnar O'Grady and a host of others, real, half-real, and imaginary—including Carl Van Vechten. Even Tallulah Bankhead, "an animated young blonde," has a walk-on in *Parties*.

Van Vechten's glamor, however, was located in New York and Paris. America was a kind of nostalgic dream, pleasant enough at a distance but deadly to meet face to face, lying vaguely between the cosmopolitan activity of New York and its pretentious imitation on the West Coast. When he approached Hollywood, he changed his tone from sophisticated comedy to burlesque. His jibes at the movies began in *The Blind Bow-Boy* with Campaspe's advice to Harold Prewett to try the movies because he is such a poor actor: "You have a good appearance, and if you were a good actor you couldn't get into the pictures." Practically all of Chapter Twelve in the same novel is satire—flimsy and weak for Van Vechten—of the movies. *Spider Boy* is, of course, his most amus-

2. The Continental charm of the novels by this author (actual name Dikran Kouyoumdjian, a British Armenian born in Bulgaria) made them best sellers on both sides of the Atlantic. The quotation is from *Mayfair*, by Michael Arlen, copyright 1925 by Doubleday and Company, Inc.

ing and devastating burlesque of Hollywood art and celebrity, and the same tone of farce runs through *Parties* in the presence of a movie queen named Midnight Blue.

He catches the Twenties' need for excitement in his novels much more surely than he does the symptoms displayed in celebrity-worship and false glamor, however. His books are a running battle against the ennui that Ulick Invern and the Twenties dreaded. They left a record of the whole feverish cycle that defied a reckoning in its pursuit of the momentary thrill. The frivolous youth and gay abandon of *Peter Whiffle* and *The Blind Bow-Boy* were products of the rising fever, anticipating rather than reporting the crest. They were self-contained, certain of their power over the inevitable shadows of existence. They announced that life could be lived forever on the plateaus of pleasure; like Frances Alda, who wrote it bluntly into her autobiography, they asserted, "I refuse to know bores. My world is active and amusing; sometimes exciting; never dull." As early as *Firecrackers*, though, Van Vechten touched the end of the dream that *Parties* made manifest, when Paul Moody was discovered at the outset musing disconsolately over his boredom: "That is the whole trouble with us damned, restless spirits, there are no new overmastering emotions .... There is nothing new to think, or to feel, or to do. Even unhappiness has become a routine tremor."

7. *THE MORAL "FREEDOM"* of the jazz age has been much discussed and perhaps too often maligned. It is simple to condemn the irresponsible liberties of an era which indulged its appetite for sensation, without considering the value of the moral revolution that made such indulgence possible. Hand in hand with the social revolution which followed World War I came a new faith in the objective revelations of science. With scientific immunity, inquiry could be made into areas of social existence which previously had been forbidden territory. The science of psychology, with Dr. Freud's theories and methods in the lead, explored the natural impulses within the dynamics of the self, and at-

tempted to discover patterns of social behavior that were inherent in the individual, heedless of those artificially imposed by folk custom and tradition except as they indicated whatever was basic and natural. The possibilities of self-knowledge and emotional maturity had never been so close at hand before. The difficulties of the age which first tasted the benefits of this release from taboo and superstition came from society's acceptance of the methods as an end rather than a means. The lag between the discoveries of science and the formation of a social philosophy which can assure their benefits to society has been the problem of more than one decade in our century. In the Fifties, the products of atomic research have placed the problem inescapably before us, and we recognize that survival now depends on our ability to deal successfully with the lag. Morally, the Twenties were the victims of circumstance. That they ignored the lag so blithely is their greatest sin.

To begin with, they attempted to re-establish a taboo in order to bring about a balance. The noble experiment of Prohibition only inspired further rebellion in a society encouraged to escape arbitrary restriction.

Sex, the most intriguing area from which the "No Trespassing" sign had been removed, became a public thoroughfare, a short-cut with the hazards of the road eliminated and the beauty of the landscape obscured by sensational billboards. By 1929, Joseph Wood Krutch lamented in *The Modern Temper*, "Love is becoming gradually so accessible, so unmysterious, and so free that its value is trivial." A year later, D. H. Lawrence, himself a serious dealer in the Freudian art, attacked the illegitimate "sex-free" "emancipated bohemians" in his essay, "Pornography and Obscenity": "The dirty little secret is no secret to him or her .... They have apparently killed the dirty little secret, but somehow they have killed everything else too .... Hence the terrible dreariness and depression of modern Bohemia, and the inward dreariness and emptiness of so many young people today."

As a consequence, marriage and the American family went through a period of severe trial. The group, in this popular philosophy, was placed second to the individual. Responsibility was centered in the ego and its urges. Sentiment could be ignored momentarily and betrayed permanently in the process. Pulled apart at the same time by entertainments available outside the home tailored to the taste of each individual in the family, and by the rising independence of women in default of the traditional double standard, the home was subject to strains which threatened even this most secure of social units.

Van Vechten's fiction reflects each of these problems with his customary give-and-take ambivalence. He reserved comment on Prohibition, virtually ignoring both its motives and its manifestations, as, indeed, most of America had, until *Parties*. There it was offered as an integral part of the tragedy of the whole decade. American Prohibition was sketched for an astonished German noblewoman who immediately yearned to witness it in action. The report she received observed that, "Other nations controlled the output of intoxicating liquors, deriving much revenue therefrom, and some nations, notably England, stipulated hours for drinking, but as drinking was prohibited in America, the government derived no benefit from the extraordinary amount of gins, wines, and whiskey consumed and one could drink wherever and whatever and whenever one pleased." For the characters who haunted American speakeasies, crowded in upon themselves in their attempt to escape, liquor was their only means.

The escape in *Parties* was persistent and insistent. After the first sober interlude in eighty pages, David Westlake admits to his wife, "We're shattered, Rilda. What we need is a drink. It's pretty near lunch time. We've had too much sober sleep. We're not used to it. The sun's too bright." When David temporarily forsakes drink in a vain attempt to stop the whirl of their existence, he asks the questions that worried a whole society in uneasy transition: "Have I stopped drinking so that I may capture some feeling out of thought, or shall I drink again to capture thought out of feeling? How exactly should I behave as a sober person?"

In matters of sex, Van Vechten's novels were notoriously emancipated. *Peter Whiffle* was uninhibited, but maintained a decorous charm in what the readers of 1922 called its indiscretions. *The Blind Bow-Boy*, however, treated even the perversions of sex with a flippant intimacy that was shocking in 1923 and still seems the least palatable of his erotic trivia.

The reputation of *The Tattooed Countess* has been celebrated by Sinclair Lewis's *Gideon Planish* in a fictitious episode that turns on the contemporary reception of its "improprieties." *Firecrackers* employs the peccadillos of the *Bow-Boy* to more serious purposes. *Nigger Heaven* and *Spider Boy* continue this trend, the first exploiting the author's most erotic sequences for both artistic and moral ends, and the second passing over them so lightly that entertaining innuendo carries the weight of the author's purpose. *Parties*, once again, is the most searching treatment of a social ill. Sex is rampant and free in this final book, but its consequences for the characters and for the reader are deeply disturbing. The frustrated lives caught in the conventions which grew out of a revolt against earlier conventions are tragically lost in a new transition. As George Dangerfield discerned, *Parties* was a significant hail-and-farewell, the manner of its author familiar, but the emotion and strength behind it more powerful than it had been in any previous book; ". . . it is painful and violent and essentially moral; and because of it Van Vechten is more definitely creative than before, and the reading of his *Parties* is an experience, not an entertainment."

Van Vechten's novels are peculiarly childless. Only two children are given speaking roles in the seven books, and each of them is unique. Consuelo Everest of *Firecrackers* is so modern and sophisticated that her mother (whom she addresses "Maman") despairs of catching up with her; in these respects, the child surpasses everyone else on the scene but Campaspe Lorillard. Regent Westlake, the other, enters the final chapter of *Parties* with no previous hint of his existence, to ask in eight-year-old confusion that Hamish Wilding try to keep his mother and father from drinking so much. "His point of view is pretty regular," Hamish remarks to a companion who, like the reader, hadn't even known David and Rilda had a child. "Of course they scarcely ever do see him because they hate to have him see them drunk and they almost always are."

Aside from these two, children are either non-existent or offstage. Campaspe and Cupid Lorillard have two boys, but they are kept at the comfortable distance of a boarding school so that their mother can escape the responsibilities and bother of having them under foot. Her marriage, appropriately, has been maintained since their birth solely as a convenience and a means of financing her extravagant whims. She has declared herself free of all encumbering affection and responsibility, and insists that her husband leave her alone. What he does, in turn, is no concern of hers: "I don't care in the least what you do. I should never have married you if I had planned to worry about you." Even the children seem to be free of any need for parental concern or affection. Cupid is a normally solicitous father, but they prefer the remote, detached Campaspe.

This wish to lead a weightless existence free from distracting alliances is almost thematic in Van Vechten's tales. It appeared first in *Peter Whiffle*, where it is even applied to friendship, which unfortunately entails "responsibility, that great god whose existence burdens our lives." Only the more realistic scenes of *The Tattooed Countess* and *Nigger Heaven* present marriage and the home as anything more than a means of placing amusing or contrasting personalities in juxtaposition, and even these books, along with the perpetual crisis of the Westlakes' marriage in *Parties*, describe tragic misunderstanding within the constraint of the family unit.

Van Vechten's personal experience seems to have only a little in common with these elements in his novels. His reminiscent essays indicate a warm affection for his sympathetic mother and a sincere admiration and respect for his father, but that is the twentieth century reflecting on the nineteenth. His own first marriage, to an early acquaintance from Cedar Rapids, terminated in divorce, but his subsequent marriage to Fania Marinoff was one of the few successful and permanent unions of their set, lasting and deepening through and beyond the turbulent Twenties.

8. THE WORLD OF BUSINESS was peripheral in Van Vechten's range of vision. That it produced the money which could be spent by the sophisticated leisure class was sufficient. When someone spoke of tired American business men, Campaspe countered, "Is there such a thing as a business man in America? I suppose so. Cupid, even, does something down town. But we try to keep that sort of thing in the background. We try not to be aware of it. It is the smart thing to do nothing, or, at any rate, to appear to do nothing." It was too commonplace to suit the public's desire for novelty. Whatever was familiar lacked the glamor required to command attention.

But when Paul Moody, to whom business was totally unfamiliar, went to work for a brokerage firm to escape the boredom of his desuetude in *Firecrackers,* he discovered the same sense of thrill and excitement there that he had sought in the company of Campaspe's depraved derelicts. He was amazed to find that they were having an extraordinarily good time.

> To be sure, they dashed nimbly after the dollar, but even that part of the game resembled gambling or fox-hunting. It was an adventure replete with thrills, false trials, happy discoveries, comic coincidences. There was so much, indeed, of sportsman's luck in everything that went on there that Wall Street was prone to impress him as a kind of glorified Monte Carlo, the Circassian walnut cabinets in each office, stored with liquors and tobacco, supplying the place of the bar, while the Stock Exchange made an excellent substitute for the salle de jeu.

It was Van Vechten's only glimpse of the American capitalistic business man, and, characteristically, he saw it only from his own limited point of view. It was glib and it was superficial, but like so many of Van Vechten's amused observations, it caught an essential spirit and an essential weakness of the era.

9. BEFORE the First World War, racial hostility had been decreasing in the United States under the influence of agencies for co-operation and understanding. The work of Booker T. Washington at Tuskegee was the most important pre-war contribution. The Southern Sociological Congress had been active since 1912. The University Commission on the Southern Race Problem, organized by James H. Dillard, studied the Negro's difficulties. The college Y.M.C.A. served as an outlet for the work of Dr. Willis D. Weatherford, president of Southern College. Recognition for the Negro had never been so promising. During the war and its aftermath, however, the nation was plunged into the most difficult period in race relationship since the Reconstruction. Violence marked the return of the Ku Klux Klan, assisted perhaps in its revival by the widely viewed movie *The Birth of a Nation,* which featured scenes of Negro terrorism in the Civil War South.

In addition, the steady migration of the Negro had spread the responsibility for his welfare and treatment. The race was growing and expanding, and the problem became less and less one of sectionalism. Dwight Dumond's *America in Our Time* records that between 1910 and 1920, "Negro urban population increased 397,000 in the South, while the rural population decreased 233,000. It increased 479,000 in the North during the same period. The movement was both northward and to industrial centers." In terms of population, in terms of geography, in terms of economic necessity, in terms of social preference, and in terms of the growing spirit of the American Negro, this was symbolized for the period by one word: Harlem.

It was from Harlem that the Negro renaissance of the Twenties came, from the forces working within for expression, and also from those aware of the accomplishment of the Negro calling its merit to the attention of the rest of America. The Negro magazines *Opportunity* and *Crisis* (the organ of the N.A.A.C.P.) encouraged and published the writings of talented Negroes, giving many of them their first chance at publication. But this was intramural recognition. Encouraged as it was by the prize competitions offered through the generosity of Amy and Joel Spingarn, it still was ingrown achievement stifled at the color line. What was needed, and what Carl Van Vechten provided with *Nigger Heaven* and the introduction-at-large of Harlem to America, was an awareness beyond Harlem of its intellect, its art, its spirit, and its talented individuals. In an age which celebrated the colorful individual, an acquaintance with one accomplished Negro meant more for racial relations than the remote work of any devoted committee. Even today, it is the Negro who has won the respect and the affection of the American public who best serves the acceptance of his race. And Van Vechten is still introducing Negro personalities as individuals, as artists, as people worthy of artistic familiarity and perpetuation, although he uses his camera now where his pen served in the past. Many Van Vechten photographs, for instance, illustrate the August, 1942, issue of *Theatre Arts,* the entire copy of which was given to "The Negro in the American Theatre."

Many Americans first found out about the struggle, the strata, and the sincerity of Harlem in *Nigger Heaven;* sensation they had already anticipated there. Once again but with more purpose and effect than ever before, a Van Vechten book reflected American society while commenting upon it. The novel was sensational enough to arouse controversy and extend its audience, but it was serious and purposeful enough to bring about an awareness of cultivated activity and blighted opportunity in Harlem. It stimulated the vogue of visiting Harlem for the rest of New York's society, a fad that brought white and black together—not always amicably, but at least together where they could see for themselves.

Van Vechten reversed the technique by bringing Harlem to New York in his celebrated parties of the Twenties. He saw no reason to distinguish color in writing invitations, and all his varied guests benefited. Langston Hughes has listed a number of New York whites who had Negro guests, but adds, ". . . only Carl Van Vechten's parties were *so* Negro that they were reported as a matter of course in the colored society columns." These parties often provided the amusement of strange assortments that always pleased Van Vechten, as well as bringing Negro and white to a point of intimate appreciation. Hughes tells of one party at which Bessie Smith sang the blues. "And when she finished, Margarita [Marguerite] D'Alvarez of the Metropolitan Opera arose and sang an aria. Bessie Smith did not know D'Alvarez, but, liking her voice, she went up to her when she had ceased and cried: 'Don't let nobody tell you you can't sing!' "

In a way, seeking recognition for the Negro has been a profession for Van Vechten. In the Twenties particularly, when intolerance was violent and widespread, it was a sincere dedication to principle and belief that attacked and eventually *denied* the color line. But if it has been anything of a profession, it has succeeded because of its total lack of any pose suggesting professional humanitarianism. It is not the work of "do-goodism," but of Peter Whiffle's "do what you have to do." Consistently, it has afforded him more pleasures than it has difficulties. He is the intimate friend of many Negroes, but it would be more exact to say merely that he is the intimate of many. He has expressed it better in his remark to George Schuyler, "I'd like it to be—well, like my house. Colored people come in and out, play an important role in my life—but there is no problem. Just people." Schuyler is the Negro writer and friend who wrote without a shade of misgiving that "Carl Van Vechten . . . has done more than any single person in this country to create the atmosphere of acceptance of the Negro."

Langston Hughes has said the same thing without the warranted but ill-fitting tone of proclamation:

> He never talks grandiloquently about democracy or Americanism. Nor makes a fetish of those qualities. But he lives them with sincerity and humor. Perhaps that is why *his* parties were reported in the Harlem press.

10. HIS AFFECTION FOR HARLEM, and intimacy with its environment, however significant it came to be, was only one facet of Van Vechten's regard for, and curiosity about, New York City. To James Huneker's Mona Milton in *Painted Veils,* it was "this salty, chill and cruel city; a Venice of receded seas, a spun-steel Venice, sans hope, sans faith, sans vision." To Sherwood Anderson it had something of the same counterfeit cosmopolitanism. He approached it as a metropolitan cynosure, a citadel constructed of the cosmopolitan wish, by beginning his chapter on "New York in the '20's" in his *Memoirs,* "O Mecca, O dream of youth, O Athens, Ohio, O Rome, O Springfield, Illinois." To Van Vechten it was all this and more, enough to convince him that "I shall never be able to do New York justice: I love her too much and I am too inconstant to any one part of her." This concluded eight pages of colorful awe and approval in the 1919 essay that summed up New York as "a subtle, banal, charming, vulgar, adorable city which has seen more civilizations in fifty years than Rome in the whole of her career, a palimpsest of human impressions, a seething furnace of every passion, every desire, a congeries of every race, every creed, stratum after stratum of new birth growing from the old."

As the focal point of glamor, sophistication, celebrity, and variety (the movies and the ubiquitous radio wave were yet to share its position), New York was at the heart of the American social personality in the Twenties. Van Vechten was a kind of first citizen of its realm, absorbing the tremendous contrasts, cataloguing its infinite variety, and taking into his own personality as its indefatigable student and observer the metropolitan air it bred and breathed. New York City was one of the most remarkable characters in his books, sometimes separate as a physical entity, more often present as a state of mind and spirit. It was, in many particulars, both the model and the picture, for the city itself often imitated Van Vechten's conception of it. Alice B. Toklas observed this in a 1951 letter to Van Vechten in which she wrote of "you and Avery [Hopwood] as creators of modern New York. You brought it up to date and then with genius pushed it way into the future, so that whatever it may be today is due to the direction and color you gave it." Others have written of the portraiture of New York in his books. H. B. Fuller, discussing *Firecrackers,* concluded: "Mr. Van Vechten will doubtless leave any metropolitan epic to other pens, but his own seems equal to turning the peculiar lyrics that the 'time' and 'place'—to borrow the language of the playbill—alike call for." In praise of Van Vechten's second novel, Ernest Boyd wrote, ". . . one turns from 'The Blind Bow-Boy' with as definite an impression of New York in 1922 as one gets of Paris under the Second Empire from the endless tomes of the Rougon Macquart series."

When Van Vechten left New York, he took it with him. Emily Clark pictures him at a country estate one summer, "sitting, detached and metropolitan, on the grass." He told her, " 'Every time I leave New York I regret it,' " adding that " 'Probably from now on pilgrims will be obliged to come to *me*.' This is spoken in no spirit of arrogance," Emily Clark remarks, "only one of decision after recollection and experience."

There has been a bond of mutual service and appreciation between Van Vechten and his city. It has given him the variety, the amusement, the art, the personalities and the milieu that his existence demands, and he has bestowed upon it these same things in return. While it has entertained him and maintained his spirit and belief in life, he has returned the vital service by contributing to its entertainment, its spirit, and its life, giving as a practical humanitarian some of the service he had received from its humanity. His voluntary service with the Stage Door Canteen during World War II is a notable instance. The mimeographed organ of that agency reported, "Carl Van Vechten does a wonderful job as head of the personnel who greet our guests, finds partners for the gals, and in addition turns up with top entertainment from out of his left sleeve."

In the Twenties, particularly, he was a kind of composite voice for New York, chronicling simultaneously what it was, what it wished to be, and what it might become.

11. THE ONE-WORD TITLE of Van Vechten's last novel symbolized perhaps the most typical manifestation of the Twenties' demand for diversion. Parties gave society personal and vital occasions for escape, occasions through which the moment could be filled with the amusement, the excitement, the tension and the challenge of personalities at close quarters. Time and life were measured in terms of these spirited entertainments; time spent not at a party was time spent in impatient anticipation of one. What *Parties* recorded in 1930 was the violent anachronism of this habitual escape at a time when escape was no longer possible. The bewilderment and disenchantment of the party-goers at the end of the decade is the undertone of tragedy that is heard like an insistent pedal point beneath the capricious scherzo of their parties. It is very much the same stark disappointment and shock that meet a person who has escaped in the artificial darkness of a matinee to the high life of the stage or screen, when he steps out of the theater into the glaring reality of daylight and the ant-like scramble of the city street. But while the performance went on inside, it was quite a show.

Van Vechten, who directed and attended more than his share of these affairs, has written reflectively of them:

> The Twenties were famous for parties; everybody both gave and went to them; there was always plenty to eat and drink, lots of talk and certainly a good deal of lewd behavior. Bob Chandler, artist and inspirer of the classical phrase, "Who's loony now?" lived next door to us on Nineteenth Street in a house where he held his celebrated entertainments, one of which a well-known actress hit off in the phrase, "I went there in the evening a young girl and came away in the early morning an old woman." Although Bob occupied an entire house, he gave his parties on the top floor, adjacent to our sixth floor apartment next door. Reasonably, I got in the habit of accepting his invitations. Occasionally there were fights. In these more circumspect days, when food and liquor are too expensive to serve lightly, it is difficult to conceive the impact of these drunken revels in the Twenties.

Van Vechten's own parties rivalled those of his notorious neighbor, perhaps surpassing them in the host's selection of his casts. Many guests have written of his affairs and all recall them with affection as well as amazement. Robert Morss Lovett has said in his autobiography, *All Our Years,* that his student and friend brought him some of the "richest experiences" in his life. His reference was partly to reading experiences shared, but it emphasized meeting Elinor Wylie and being introduced to much of Van Vechten's cosmopolitan society. Nancy Hoyt, in her biography of her sister, Elinor Wylie, wrote of her 1923 experience, "Bill [Benét] and Elinor took me to friends' like Carl Van Vechten's, where there were people like Carl and Fania, and things like cats and pictures and books and drinks and cigarettes of such superb quality and elegance...."

But these were earlier glimpses before the cultivated salon had become an antic saloon. Later, the gatherings took on speed and dropped any remaining ballast of reserve. The colorful story about Van Vechten parties in the Savoy in London, "in which, it was said, Van Vechten took several floors of the hotel, stocked them with liquors and vintage wines, and held open house for days and nights," although it was apocryphal, gave some indication of the pace.[3] As readers of *Parties* we recall David Westlake's personal fog in the London sequences. Langston Hughes remembers "a gossip party, where everybody was at liberty to go around the room repeating the worst things they could make up or recall about each other to their friends on opposite sides of the room— who were sure to go right over and tell them all about it." Hughes adds a picture of the host at these frivolous occasions: "Carl Van Vechten moved about filling glasses and playing host with the greatest of zest at his parties, while his tiny wife, Fania Marinoff, looking always very pretty and very gay, when the evening grew late would sometimes take Mr. Van Vechten severely to task for his drinking—before bidding the remaining guests good night and retiring to her bed." In a letter to Emily Clark, Van Vechten reported gleefully one of the most memorable accounts of his parties. Written on shipboard, it stated, "I am occupying part of the royal suite on the *Mauretania* and my going-away party was sensational. There was lots of champagne and I am sure the personnel of the ship must have decided that Booker T. Washington was sailing. Nora Holt sang 'My Daddy Rocks Me' in the last moments."

This event catches the flavor of both of the capitalized adjectives in what Van Vechten has referred to as "the splendid Drunken Twenties,

3. Van Vechten reports that he never gave a party at the Savoy. The quotation is from *We Were Interrupted,* by Burton Rascoe. Copyright 1947 by Burton Rascoe, reprinted by permission of Doubleday and Company, Inc.

the speakeasy era when ladies wore the ugly hip-waisted, short dresses." For what was significant and unique beyond the hilarity, the freedom, and the naughtiness of these episodes, was an attractive gregariousness and congeniality. In Van Vechten's parties this was marked by the strange casts that brought together characters, personalities, talents, and races, all equalized and brilliantly highlighted in the cordiality and the confinement of an apartment, an evening, and an appreciative host. This was the quality that made his entertainments memorable and fabulous rather than ephemeral and merely fabled. This is the individual note that predominates in Emily Clark's memory of a "June evening in Carl's apartment."

> ... with George Gershwin at the piano playing and singing bits from his current musical show to a crowd of people, among whom Theodore Dreiser sat, heavy and brooding, the direct antithesis, almost a contradiction of all that Gershwin means. And Elinor Wylie sat, aloof and lovely, a contradiction and denial of all that both Dreiser and Gershwin mean. Later some woman danced, and later still Paul Robeson sang. Last of all, James Weldon Johnson recited his 'Go Down, Death.' And Carl hovered about in doorways, his face, as always on such evenings, benevolent and shining. ... The gold-fish is swimming happily and unconsciously in his own proper element. Everyone is at peace. And these people are gaily giving their best work for nothing; or, rather, for Carl.

Van Vechten still has parties and he still thrives in the animated atmosphere of New York, but his amusements and his activities and his life are modulated to suit the demands of the present. There is no anachronism about his active presence in an America three decades removed in time from *Peter Whiffle,* for Carl still honors Peter's discovery that "it is necessary to do only what one must, what one is forced by nature to do." He continues more and more to offer his service as humanitarian and appreciative observer, and he continues to enjoy immensely the people and the world about him. The vitality and the capacity for pleasure which marked the Twenties are still a part of Van Vechten, but the irresponsibilities of that era are behind him. When he emerged from the darkened theater and the ten-year matinee of amusement and escape, he realized he had seen a last performance. But he brought along with him into the sober daylight of succeeding years some of its most serviceable and memorable scenes.

Later decades may well censure the wayward emphasis of an era that set out, as every era does in its own way, to conquer boredom through some appealing pattern of life. But there is a certain element of inevitability that conditions the choice. If they had been choosing in 1920, or 1925, or even 1928, the chances are they would have chosen the same riotous pattern. They may not, however, have had the impudent honesty or the careless foresight to echo Peter Whiffle's impertinent defense of his folly, "It was all gay, irresponsible and meaningless, perhaps, but *gay*."

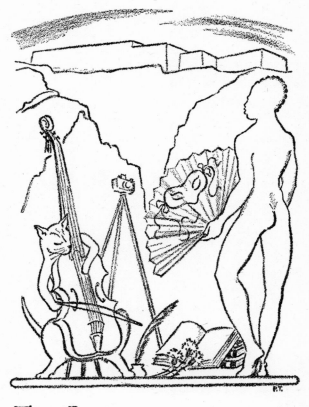

Ex Libris
Carl Van Vechten

A CHRONOLOGY OF BOOKS by Carl Van Vechten

1915	Music After the Great War
1916	Music and Bad Manners
1917	Interpreters and Interpretations
1918	The Merry-Go-Round
1918	The Music of Spain
1920	In the Garret
1920	Interpreters
1920	The Tiger in the House
1922	Peter Whiffle: His Life and Works
1923	The Blind Bow-Boy
1924	The Tattooed Countess
1925	Red
1925	Firecrackers
1926	Excavations
1926	Nigger Heaven
1928	Spider Boy
1930	Feathers
1930	Parties
1932	Sacred and Profane Memories

All of Carl Van Vechten's books were published by Alfred A. Knopf, with the exception of his first book of essays, *Music After the Great War*, which was published by G. Schirmer.

VAN VECHTEN'S BOOKPLATE, DESIGNED BY PRENTISS TAYLOR

Klaus Jonas has compiled *Carl Van Vechten, A Bibliography,* New York: Alfred A. Knopf, 1955.

Carl Van Vechten has established special collections at three libraries: Fisk University has his Florine Stettheimer Memorial Collection of Books About the Fine Arts and his George Gershwin Memorial Collection of Music and Musical Literature. The Yale University Library has his Anna Marble Pollack Memorial Library of Books About Cats as well as the expanding James Weldon Johnson Memorial Collection of Negro Arts and Letters. To the New York Public Library he has given The Carl Van Vechten Collection, his manuscripts and personal correspondence annotated by their donor.

SELECTED LIST OF RELATED READINGS

MUSIC AND THE ARTS

ALDA, FRANCES. *Men, Women and Tenors.* Boston: Houghton Mifflin Company, 1937.

ARMITAGE, MERLE. *Accent on America.* New York: E. Weyhe, 1944.

"CARL VAN VECHTEN," *Cue* (April 9, 1949), pp. 18-19.

EWEN, DAVID. *Music Comes to America.* New York: Allen, Towne and Heath, 1947.

FARRAR, GERALDINE. *Such Sweet Compulsion.* New York: The Greystone Press, 1938.

FINKLESTEIN, SIDNEY. *Jazz: A People's Music.* New York: The Citadel Press, 1948.

FRENCH, RICHARD F. (ed.). *Music and Criticism, A Symposium.* Cambridge: Harvard University Press, 1948.

GILMAN, LAWRENCE. *The Music of Tomorrow.* New York: John Lane Company, 1907.

——————. *Phases of Modern Music.* New York: Harper and Brothers, 1904.

HANDY, W. C. *Father of the Blues.* New York: The Macmillan Company, 1941.

Huneker, James Gibbons. *Bedouins.* New York: Charles Scribner's Sons, 1920.

—————. *Mezzotints in Modern Music.* New York: Charles Scribner's Sons, 1899.

—————. *Steeplejack.* New York: Charles Scribner's Sons, 1920.

Larkin, Oliver W. *Art and Life in America.* New York: Rinehart and Company, 1949.

Lueders, Edward G. "Music Criticism in America," *American Quarterly,* III (Summer, 1951), 142-151.

Mason, Daniel Gregory. *Contemporary Composers.* New York: The Macmillan Company, 1918.

—————. *The Dilemma of American Music.* New York: The Macmillan Company, 1928.

Mencken, Henry L. "James Huneker," *A Book of Prefaces.* New York: Garden City Publishing Company, 1927.

Newman, Ernest. *A Musical Critic's Holiday.* New York: Alfred A. Knopf, 1925.

Parker, Henry T. *Eighth Notes.* New York: Dodd, Mead and Company, 1922.

Ramsey, Russell. "Modern Tendencies in Music," *The Dial,* LXII (January 11, 1917), 21-23.

Rosenfeld, Paul. *Musical Chronicle: 1917-1923.* New York: Harcourt, Brace and Company, 1923.

Salazar, Adolfo. *Music in Our Time.* Translated by Isabel Pope. New York: W. W. Norton and Company, 1946.

Sargeant, Winthrop. *Jazz: Hot and Hybrid.* New York: E. P. Dutton and Company, 1946.

Seldes, Gilbert. *The Seven Lively Arts.* New York: Harper and Brothers, 1924.

Soubies, Alfred J. *Histoire de la Musique: Espagne.* Paris: E. Flammarion Successeur, 1900.

Thompson, Oscar. "An American School of Criticism: The Legacy Left by W. J. Henderson, Richard Aldrich and their Colleagues of the Old Guard," *Musical Quarterly,* XXIII (October, 1937), 428-433.

—————. *Practical Musical Criticism.* New York: Witmark Educational Publications, 1934.

Wright, Frank Lloyd. *An Autobiography.* London, New York: Longmans, Green and Company, 1933.

LITERATURE

ARLEN, MICHAEL. *Mayfair*. New York: George H. Doran, 1925.

BABBITT, IRVING, et al. *Criticism in America*. New York: Harcourt, Brace and Company, 1924.

BEACH, JOSEPH WARREN. *The Outlook for American Prose*. Chicago: University of Chicago Press, 1927.

CABELL, JAMES BRANCH. *Beyond Life*. New York: The Modern Library, 1923.

CARGILL, OSCAR. *Intellectual America*. New York: The Macmillan Company, 1941.

CLARK, EMILY. *Innocence Abroad*. New York: Alfred A. Knopf, 1931.

CLEATON, IRENE and ALLEN. *Books and Battles: American Literature, 1920-1930*. Boston: Houghton Mifflin Company, 1937.

FARRAR, JOHN (ed.). *The Literary Spotlight*. New York: George H. Doran, 1924.

FIRBANK, RONALD. *Five Novels*. Norfolk, Conn.: New Directions, 1949.

FITZGERALD, F. SCOTT. *The Portable F. Scott Fitzgerald*. Edited by Dorothy Parker, with an introduction by John O'Hara. New York: The Viking Press, 1945.

HUNEKER, JAMES GIBBONS. *Painted Veils*. New York: Liveright Publishing Corporation, Black and Gold Edition, 1942.

HUYSMANS, JORIS KARL. *Against the Grain [A Rebours]*. Introduction by Havelock Ellis. New York: Hartsdale House, 1931.

JACKSON, HOLBROOK. *The Eighteen Nineties*. London: Grant Richards, Limited, 1918.

KAZIN, ALFRED. *On Native Grounds*. New York: Reynal and Hitchcock, 1942.

KNOPF, ALFRED A. "Reminiscences of Hergesheimer, Van Vechten, and Mencken," *Yale University Library Gazette*, XXIV (April, 1950), 145-164.

LAWRENCE, D. H. *Phoenix: The Posthumous Papers of D. H. Lawrence*. Edited by Edward D. McDonald. New York: The Viking Press, 1936.

LEWIS, SINCLAIR. *Gideon Planish*. New York: Random House, 1943. (p. 130 et seq.)

McKay, Claude. *Home to Harlem.* New York: Harper and Brothers, 1928.

Mizener, Arthur. *The Far Side of Paradise.* Boston: Houghton Mifflin Company, 1950.

Overton, Grant. *When Winter Comes to Main Street.* New York: George H. Doran, 1922.

Richards, Grant. *Author Hunting.* New York: Coward-McCann, 1934.

Saltus, Edgar. *The Imperial Orgy.* New York: The Modern Library, 1927.

Towne, Charles Hanson, et al. *W. Somerset Maugham, Novelist, Essayist, Dramatist.* With a Note on Novel Writing by Mr. Maugham. New York: George H. Doran, n.d.

Wylie, Elinor. *The Collected Prose of Elinor Wylie.* New York: Alfred A. Knopf, 1946.

SOCIETY

Allen, Frederick Lewis. *Only Yesterday.* New York: Blue Ribbon Books, 1931.

Anderson, Sherwood. *Sherwood Anderson's Memoirs.* New York: Harcourt, Brace and Company, 1942.

Boyd, Ernest. "Aesthete: Model 1924," *American Mercury,* I (January, 1924), 51-56.

Chamberlain, John. *Farewell to Reform.* New York: Liveright, Incorporated, 1932.

Cowley, Malcolm. *Exile's Return.* New York: The Viking Press, 1951.

Dumond, Dwight Lowell. *America in Our Time, 1896-1946.* New York: Henry Holt and Company, 1947.

Eastman, Max. *Enjoyment of Living.* New York: Harper and Brothers, 1948.

Fletcher, John Gould. *Life Is My Song.* New York: Farrar and Rinehart, 1937.

Freeman, Joseph. *An American Testament.* New York: Farrar and Rinehart, 1936.

Hicks, Granville. *John Reed, The Making of a Revolutionary.* New York: The Macmillan Company, 1937.

Hughes, Langston. *The Big Sea.* New York: Alfred A. Knopf, 1940.

Jacobs, Lewis. *The Rise of the American Film.* New York: Harcourt, Brace and Company, 1939.

Johnson, Gerald W. *Incredible Tale.* New York: Harper and Brothers, 1950.

JOHNSON, JAMES WELDON. *Along This Way*. New York: The Viking Press, 1933.

KEMLER, EDGAR. *The Irreverent Mr. Mencken*. Boston: Little, Brown and Company, 1950.

KRUTCH, JOSEPH WOOD. *The Modern Temper*. New York: Harcourt, Brace and Company, 1929.

LEIGHTON, ISABEL (ed.). *The Aspirin Age, 1919-1941*. New York: Simon and Schuster, 1949.

LIPPMANN, WALTER. *A Preface to Morals*. New York: The Macmillan Company, 1929.

LOVETT, ROBERT MORSS. *All Our Years*. New York: The Viking Press, 1948.

LUHAN, MABEL DODGE. *European Experiences*. Volume II of *Intimate Memories*. New York: Harcourt, Brace and Company, 1935.

——————. *Movers and Shakers*. Volume III of *Intimate Memories*. New York: Harcourt, Brace and Company, 1936.

MERZ, CHARLES. *The Dry Decade*. Garden City, New York: Doubleday, Doran and Company, 1932.

MORRIS, LLOYD. *Postscript to Yesterday; America: The Last Fifty Years*. New York: Random House, 1947.

MUMFORD, LEWIS. *Technics and Civilization*. New York: Harcourt, Brace and Company, 1934.

PARRY, ALBERT. *Garrets and Pretenders: A History of Bohemianism in America*. New York: Covici, Friede, 1933.

RASCOE, BURTON. *We Were Interrupted*. Garden City: Doubleday and Company, 1947.

SCHUYLER, GEORGE S. *The Van Vechten Revolution*. Reprinted from *Phylon*, The Atlanta University Review of Race and Culture (Fourth Quarter, 1950). Atlanta: n.d.

STEARNS, HAROLD E. (ed.). *Civilization in the United States*. New York: Harcourt, Brace and Company, 1922.

STEIN, GERTRUDE. *The Autobiography of Alice B. Toklas*. New York: Harcourt, Brace and Company, 1933. (Random House).

SULLIVAN, MARK. *The Twenties*. Volume VI of *Our Times*. New York: Charles Scribner's Sons, 1926.

WARE, CAROLINE. *Greenwich Village, 1920-1930*. Boston: Houghton Mifflin Company, 1935.

WHITE, WILLIAM ALLEN. *A Puritan in Babylon: The Story of Calvin Coolidge*. New York: The Macmillan Company, 1938.

INDEX

and the Twenties